DAILY READINGS FROM
YOUR
Best Life
NOW

DAILY READINGS FROM

YOUR *BEST LIFE* NOW

90 DEVOTIONS FOR LIVING AT YOUR FULL POTENTIAL

JOEL OSTEEN

New York   Boston   Nashville

Scriptures noted NIV are taken from the HOLY BIBLE: NEW INTERNATIONAL VERSION®. Copyright © 1973, 1978, 1984 by International Bible Society. Used by permission of Zondervan Publishing House. All rights reserved.

Scriptures noted NKJV are taken from THE NEW KING JAMES VERSION. Copyright © 1979, 1980, 1982, Thomas Nelson, Inc., Publishers.

Scriptures noted NASB are from the NEW AMERICAN STANDARD BIBLE®. Copyright © 1960, 1962, 1963, 1968, 1971, 1972, 1973, 1975, 1977, 1995 by The Lockman Foundation. Used by permission.

Scriptures noted THE MESSAGE are from *THE MESSAGE*. Copyright © 1993, 1994, 1995, 1996, 2000, 2001, 2002. Used by permission of NavPress Publishing Group.

Scriptures noted TLB are from *The Living Bible,* copyright © 1971. Used by permission of Tyndale House Publishers, Inc., Wheaton, Illinois 60189. All rights reserved.

Scriptures noted NLT are from the *Holy Bible,* New Living Translation, copyright © 1996. Used by permission of Tyndale House Publishers, Inc., Wheaton, Illinois 60189. All rights reserved.

Scriptures noted KJV are from the KING JAMES VERSION of the Holy Bible.

Scriptures noted AMP are from THE AMPLIFIED BIBLE: Old Testament. Copyright © 1962, 1964 by Zondervan Publishing House (used by permission); and from THE AMPLIFIED NEW TESTAMENT. Copyright © 1958 by the Lockman Foundation (used by permission).

Portions of this book have been adapted from *Your Best Life Now*. Copyright © 2004 by Joel Osteen. Published by Warner Faith, Time Warner Book Group.

Warner Faith
Time Warner Book Group
1271 Avenue of the Americas, New York, NY 10020
Visit our Web site at www.twbookmark.com.

The Warner Faith name and logo are registered trademarks of the Time Warner Book Group.

Printed in the United States of America
First Warner Faith printing: October 2005
10 9 8 7 6 5 4 3 2 1
ISBN: 0-446-57810-X
LCCN: 2005927858

INTRODUCTION

PRACTICAL WAYS TO BEGIN LIVING YOUR BEST LIFE NOW

I WAS SEATED at a bookstore table in Chicago, signing copies of *Your Best Life Now* for a long line of patient people, when I looked up and saw two women, arm in arm, standing in front of me. One woman looked to be in her early thirties; the other was apparently her mother. Their eyes were slightly red and puffy, as though they had been crying recently.

When they told me their story, I understood their tears. They were indeed mother and daughter, but they had been estranged from each other for more than twelve years. Although they both lived in the Chicago area, they had not spoken to each other for that length of time.

Each of them had read *Your Best Life Now* and came to the store that day for an autograph. At the bookstore, they saw each other for the first time in more than a decade. They discovered that they both had changed, and they had a tearful reunion.

"Thank you for writing this book," one of the women said. "It not only created the opportunity for our reconciliation, but it transformed our lives to the point where we were able to forgive the past and move forward. Your book changed our lives."

What a privilege it has been for me to hear that sentence again and again as people who have read *Your Best Life Now* have spoken or written to me. They have told me how God has used that book to positively impact their lives or the lives of people close to them. Many have shared incidents in which they put the principles to the test, and discovered (sometimes to their surprise) that these biblical truths really helped them to achieve their full potential.

Others have said, "Joel, there's just so much information in *Your Best Life Now*. Each chapter is filled with important concepts that I want to practice in my life."

Consequently, many have expressed a desire to work through the power-packed principles more slowly, taking "bite-sized bits," studying the scriptural foundations upholding them, analyzing these truths, and applying them to their personal situations. To help in that process, I am delighted to offer *Daily Readings from Your Best Life Now*.

A "devotional" is not meant to be an exhaustive treatment of a particular passage of Scripture; instead, it is intended to inspire ardent love and worship of God. It's my desire that the selections I've chosen to emphasize will be keys you can use to unlock doors leading to a fuller life. This devotional extracts many of the stories and principles contained in my book and organizes them in daily doses.

Combined with an appropriate Scripture reading that sheds light on the main idea for that selection and a key Bible passage (which you might want to consider memorizing), the material is assembled in such a way as to make it ideal for your own personal spiritual growth. Each selection serves as a springboard to help you draw nearer to God and to help you overcome the obstacles that might keep you from living your best life now. A suggested prayer is included at the end of each selection to help you express your heart's desires, your prayer requests, and fresh commitments to God. Obviously, your prayers are as important to God as mine are, so don't feel confined to the suggested prayer. It is simply a place to start in your communication with your heavenly Father.

Take your time as you work through these pages. This book is not meant to be consumed at one reading or even within a few days. It is intended to be a three-month program that will give you a fresh outlook on life, establishing within you such vibrantly new perspectives, you may never be the same. Read one devotional each day for ninety days. Think about the main point of that devotional throughout the day, and allow it to be a catalyst to provoke further study, thought, and contemplation of the good things that God has in store for you. Look up and read carefully each selected "Scripture Reading for Your Best Life Now." These passages will sometimes relate directly to the principle being described, and in other instances, the Scripture reading will provide necessary background for accurately understanding the truth you are studying. It is important that you don't neglect these short portions of God's Word if you want to gain the most benefit from this book.

I'm convinced that by the end of the next three months, your life can be transformed and renewed as you allow God's Word to refresh you and to reshape your thinking, speaking, and daily activities. May this devotional book be instrumental in helping you to live your best life now!

Joel Osteen

PART ONE

ENLARGE YOUR VISION

LET'S START BELIEVING FOR MORE

SCRIPTURE READING FOR YOUR BEST LIFE NOW   Hebrews 11:8–40

Now faith is the assurance of things hoped for, the conviction of things not seen.

HEBREWS 11:1 NASB

A FAMOUS MOUNTAIN-CLIMBING resort in the Swiss Alps caters to businesses that encourage their employees to hike up the mountain trails together. The goal is to build camaraderie and to teach teamwork. Although it is about an eight-hour trek to the summit, anyone with normal walking ability can ascend to the top. Each morning, the hikers gather at the base of the mountain for a pep talk before starting the climb. Usually, the group is so excited, they can hardly wait to head up the slopes, to have a group picture taken, and to celebrate their victory.

They hike for several hours before taking a break. Approximately halfway up the mountain stands a quaint alpine restaurant. About noon, the weary hikers trudge into the restaurant, peel off their hiking gear, and plop down by the fireplace to have a cup of coffee, or drink some hot chocolate, and eat their lunch. With the mountain as their backdrop, the hikers savor the warm, cozy, picturesque setting.

Interestingly, after they are full and comfortable, less than half the hikers choose to continue climbing to the top of the mountain. It isn't because they aren't able; it isn't because the climb is too dif-

ficult. Their reluctance to continue is simply because they are satisfied with where they are. They lose their drive to excel, to ex-
plore new horizons, to experience vistas they'd never previously
imagined possible. They have tasted a bit of success, and they
think, *This is good enough.*

**God has so
much more
in store.**

Many times, we do something similar. We have a goal to break a bad
habit, to lose some weight, or to pay
off our credit cards. At first, we're so
excited. We're fired up and we go after
it! But over time, we get lazy; we get
complacent. Maybe we see a little improvement, but then we get
comfortable right where we are. *Where we are* may not be a bad
place, but we know it's not where we're supposed to be. We're not
stretching our faith. We're not pursuing the excellence that God
has placed in our hearts.

"Well, Joel, I'm doing pretty well with my goal," one fellow
said. "I used to smoke two packs of cigarettes a day, and now I
smoke only one." Another person said, "I used to be fifty pounds
overweight, but I've lost ten pounds recently."

"I'm happy for you," I told these individuals. "That's a good
start, and it took some real effort to get where you are. But don't
get comfortable. Don't be satisfied with a little improvement.
Begin believing for better progress, and press on to God's best."

Maybe you own a business and you've experienced a bit of success. Lately, however, you've been coasting, thinking that perhaps
you've reached your limits. You're not stretching your faith. You
aren't believing for an increase in your customer base or your
profits. No, don't stop halfway; go on up to the top of that mountain. Believe God for more.

Dare to step out of your comfort zone today. God has so much
more in store. Keep pursuing and keep believing. It doesn't take
any more effort to believe and stay filled with faith than it takes
to develop a negative and defeated attitude. Get up every day and

say, "This is going to be a good day! I believe my dreams are coming to pass. God has great things in store." When you have that kind of attitude, you are releasing God's supernatural power in your life, and before long, you will begin experiencing more of God's goodness.

But it doesn't come easily. People who see their dreams come to pass are people who have some resolve, some backbone; people who refuse to settle for somewhere along the way. In the Old Testament, Abraham was one of the heroes of faith, a man with whom God established a covenant that still impacts the world today. Ironically, many years earlier, Abraham's father, Terah, had hoped to move to the place where God later led Abraham. The Scripture says, "Abraham's father left Ur and set out for Canaan" (see Genesis 11:31). Now Canaan was the Promised Land, and Terah had intended to lead his family to that land of abundance. But the Scripture reveals that Terah "stopped along the way and settled in Haran" (see Genesis 11:31). Why did he stop there?

No doubt it was difficult traveling with his flocks, herds, family members, and all of their possessions. You can imagine how stressful that was, not to mention what a big headache moving must have been four thousand years ago. Finally, Terah said, "I can't go any farther. I know this isn't the Promised Land, but let's just settle here; it's good enough. At least we can survive here."

I wonder how many times we do the same thing. We have a big dream in our hearts—we're going to excel in our careers, excel as parents, excel in our walk with God. We get started, but then things get difficult, and achieving our goal doesn't happen as quickly as we had hoped. Perhaps, similar to Abraham's father, we say, "Let's just settle here. It's not really what we wanted, but it's good enough."

Don't fall into that trap. You are made for more than good enough. Look yourself in the mirror and say, "I am not going to settle for mediocrity. Things may be difficult. Nothing may be going my way right now, but I'm going to keep pursuing God. I'm

going to trust God to help me expand my horizons and keep believing for all that He has for me. I'm going to make it all the way
into my Promised Land."

Maybe like Abraham's father you've already settled halfway,
and you've gotten comfortable in that spot where you are. I'm
challenging you to pull up your stakes, pack your tents, get your
belongings, and start moving forward. Enlarge your vision! You
may have had a delay, but that's okay; you can begin again this
very day. You simply need to focus on your goal, set your course,
and have the attitude, *I'm not going to settle for* a little *love and
joy*, a bit of *peace and contentment, or for* a small helping of *happiness. No, I'm going to reach my full potential in God. I'm going
to start living my best life now!*

✑ Today's Prayer for Your Best Life Now ✑

*Father, I'm excited to begin this new journey of faith with
You. Please help me to develop a fresh vision for my life, to
believe You for better days ahead, and to know that You will
continually expand my horizons as I trust You to do more in
and through my life.*

HAVING A POSITIVE VISION

The eye is the lamp of the body; so then if your eye is clear, your whole body will be full of light. But if your eye is bad, your whole body will be full of darkness.
MATTHEW 6:22–23 NASB

GOD CREATED YOU as a visual being with an incredible imagination. Your eyes take in four million bytes of information every second. The moment input reaches your brain, that data is processed, forming a 3-D color picture in your mind.

Your imagination is extremely powerful. If I write the words "big black dog," you don't simply see the words; your mind shows you an image of that animal, a picture that is drawn up from your mental computer memory banks. In the same way, each of us has a picture of ourselves in our imaginations. That "self-image" is similar to a thermostat in a room. It sets the standard at which you will function. You will never consistently rise higher than the image you have of yourself, and you will never accomplish things that you don't first see yourself accomplishing.

Unfortunately, many people have a negative vision for their lives. They don't see themselves rising higher or overcoming their obstacles. Consequently, they're limited by their own vision.

The Bible says your eye is the lamp of your body. Obviously, that is not talking about your physical sight; it's talking about what you see through your eyes of faith, your *spiritual* vision. It's talking about the type of image you're keeping in front of you. God is saying, in effect, if you focus on your problems, on what you can't do, or if you think you've already reached your limits, then that image of mediocrity will keep you stuck right where you are. It's not because God doesn't want to promote you; it's simply because you are focused on the wrong things. You're developing the wrong images in your mind.

On the other hand, if you can learn to look at life through your eyes of faith and start seeing yourself rising to new levels—seeing yourself accomplishing your dreams, receiving more, giving more, loving more, and enjoying life, seeing your family serving God— you'll experience God's blessings and favor.

We produce what we continually keep in front of us. If you keep an image of success in your mind, you're going to move toward success, but if you see yourself as barely getting by, your marriage getting worse, your health going downhill, then most likely your life will gravitate toward those negative situations.

It's a simple truth that you cannot give birth to something you have not first conceived. You must conceive it on the inside through your eyes of faith before it will come to pass on the outside. Your vision, what you see, has a tremendous impact in your life. We need to quit allowing our imaginations to keep us beaten down to where we don't think we can do anything. Instead, let's start allowing God to use our imaginations to build us up, to help us accomplish our dreams. In other words, keep things in front of you that you want to see come to pass.

Your imagination is like a canvas. You can paint on it any kind of picture you choose through your thoughts, attitudes, and what you decide to focus on. Don't let doubt or fear paint on your canvas. Don't let "impossible" or "can't be done" thoughts blur the colors on your canvas.

Instead, take out the paintbrush of faith, the paintbrush of hope, the paintbrush of expectancy and begin painting a bright future on the canvas of your heart. Understand: The kind of mental picture you paint is the goal toward which you will move. That image will set the limits for your life. If you want to change your life, you need to change the picture you're painting in your mind.

In the Old Testament, God told Abraham he was going to be the father of many nations. What's so unusual about that? Simply this: At the time God said this, Abraham didn't have any children, and he was very old, as was his wife, Sarah. In the natural, it was an impossible situation. But God gave Abraham some unusual instructions. He said, "Abraham, go outside and look up at the stars, for as many stars as you can see, that's how many descendants you are going to have" (see Genesis 15:5).

Why did God tell Abraham to go out and look up at the stars? God had already promised Abraham he was going to be a father.

God knew it wasn't enough for Abraham simply to hear it; he needed to get a picture of it in his mind. God wanted Abraham to have a visual image, to see it in his imagination. So every night when Abraham went outside and looked up, he was reminded of God's promise to him. Even though it didn't come to pass for twenty years, Abraham saw himself as the father of many nations; he saw it through his eyes of faith. He conceived it on the inside, in his heart. Abraham painted that picture on the canvas of his mind, and eventually God brought it to pass.

> Abraham saw himself as the father of many nations; he saw it through his eyes of faith.

Maybe the reason you are not experiencing God's best, the reason you may be stuck in a rut, is simply because your *vision* needs to be improved.

"Well," you say, "I've got a lot of problems. I'm really in debt," or, "I'm really lonely."

Fine, start seeing yourself the way you want to be. You may be in difficulties, you may be struggling, but don't let that image take root. Paint a new picture. Start seeing yourself rising out of your troubles. Start seeing yourself as more than a conqueror.

Maybe you have a lot of strife and division in your heart. You and your spouse are having a hard time getting along. Instead of giving up on that marriage, look through your eyes of faith and start seeing your family living in peace and harmony. Change what you're seeing, and you will change what you are producing.

✑ Today's Prayer for Your Best Life Now ✑

Beginning today, I will lift up my head and start to get a new image in my mind of the tremendous potential that You have poured into my life. Help me, Father, to paint a new picture on the canvas of my imagination, to live with faith, seeing with my spiritual eyes not just what exists today, but the life that is possible because of You.

DEVELOP A BETTER PICTURE

You have eyes—can't you see? You have ears—can't you hear? Don't you remember anything at all?

MARK 8:18 NLT

RECENTLY, A MIDDLE-AGED man told me, "Joel, I always knew I was going to get diabetes. My father had it. My grandfather had it. It's been in my family line for generations." He told me that from the time he was a teenager, he had known the day was coming when he'd hear the doctor give him that dire diagnosis. He was expecting it. He already saw himself with diabetes, and, unfortunately, he got exactly what he predicted.

Some people might think he got diabetes because he didn't have faith. No, I hate to say it, but his faith was working just fine. Do you know your faith can function negatively just as easily as it will function positively? If your family has a long history of sickness and disease, don't sit back and see yourself the same way. "Well, I guess this is my lot in life."

No, you—more than anybody else—need to start developing a new picture. You need to see yourself as strong, healthy, and living a long, satisfied life. You can be the one to break that curse of ill health. But the first thing you must do is change the image you have of yourself on the inside. Get a new vision. Make sure your eyes are filled with light.

That is what my mother did back in 1981, when she was diagnosed with terminal cancer and the doctors gave her only a few weeks to live. In my book *Your Best Life Now*, I told the story of how Mother prayed, believed, and quoted aloud passages of Scripture related to healing every day. But Mother didn't just pray. She didn't just quote the Scripture. She also put up pictures of herself all over the house—pictures taken previously at happy times in her life, when she was healthy. She put pictures in the kitchen, the living room, even in the bathroom. Everywhere she went, she saw those images of health and happiness.

Mother could easily have looked in the mirror and gotten depressed. She could have let the wrong image take root. After all, she weighed only eighty-nine pounds. She was weak, emaciated, and her skin had already turned a deathly color of yellow. But instead of dwelling on that image, Mother put up pictures in which she was vibrantly happy. I recall that in her bathroom she had a picture of herself wearing a pink cowboy hat and riding a big brown horse during a family vacation in Montana. Every time she went into that bathroom, she saw herself happy, healthy, and enjoying life. In the kitchen, she placed pictures from her wedding. In the den, she hung other photos that portrayed her as happy, strong, healthy, and living life to the full.

She refused to dwell on the negative diagnosis; she didn't focus on her sick body. She looked out through her eyes of faith, and she saw herself the way she wanted to be. Externally, she was weak and feeble, but internally, on the inside in her heart and mind, she was strong, determined, and healthy. She refused to let that weak, defeated image take root. Instead, she insisted on seeing herself as the victor and not the victim. God, in His goodness, totally healed her. She became what she saw and to this day, more than twenty years later, she's as healthy as she can be. She could even get on that big horse again if she wanted to.

Friend, you, too, will produce what you keep in front of you. What kind of pictures have you placed on the walls of your mind?

Do you see yourself getting stronger and healthier? Do you see yourself rising higher in life, accomplishing your dreams?

At my house, all around me I have pictures of things that inspire me. I like looking at beautiful sunsets. I like seeing eagles soaring in the sky. On my desk at home I have articles and letters people have written to me that have spoken faith into my life. I have pictures of our family when we were having fun together. I have a photograph of my dad and me going down the Amazon River. I like to put things in front of me that remind me of good times in the past, while expanding my vision for better experiences in the future.

In your home or office, put things up that build your faith. Put out photos that bring back good memories. Put pictures on the wall or on your desk that show you living life to the full. When you look at those pictures, don't just go by them and say, "I wish I was still that happy," or, "I wish I could still fit in that size dress," or, "I wish I still had that much hair."

No, let the image of victory take root. Get it on the inside. For many people, it helps to decorate their walls with Scripture verses. On the bathroom mirror or where you get dressed, place Scriptures such as "I can do all things through Christ" or "This is the day the Lord has made." On the refrigerator, remind yourself, "I am more than a conqueror," and "God always causes me to triumph." At the back door, place the truth "God's favor is surrounding me like a shield," or "Goodness and mercy are following me today." Put up things that build you up spiritually, keep you filled with faith, and help you to have a big vision for your life.

What kind of pictures have you placed on the walls of your mind?

Don't get stuck in a rut. Nothing may be going right for you today, but start seeing yourself rising out of it. See yourself overcoming that addiction. Envision yourself getting that promotion. Let that new image sink deep down inside you. To produce it on the outside, you must first picture it on the inside.

❧ Today's Prayer for Your Best Life Now ❧

Father, please help me to take down the negative pictures in my mind and to replace them with faith-filled photos, special memories, and images of hope for a tremendous future. I believe You want me to enlarge my vision, to expand my horizons, and to engage in a life that will have eternal significance.

IT'S TIME TO ENLARGE YOUR VISION

SCRIPTURE READING FOR YOUR BEST LIFE NOW   Matthew 9:16–17

See, I am doing a new thing! Now it springs up; do you not perceive it?

ISAIAH 43:19 NIV

EARLY IN OUR marriage, Victoria and I walked through a beautiful, partially constructed home in our neighborhood. After viewing the house, Victoria said, "Joel, one day we're going to live in a home just like that!" Visions of our bank account and my income at the time filled my mind. It seemed impossible to me that we'd ever work our way up to a home like the one we had toured. I didn't want to discourage my wife, but I didn't want her to live with unrealistic dreams either, so I replied, "Victoria, I don't see how we could ever afford something like that."

But Victoria had much more faith than I did. Before long, by speaking words of faith and victory, she convinced me that we could live in an elegant home like the one we saw. I started believing that God could bring it to pass. We kept on believing, too, seeing ourselves living in that beautiful home, even while we continued living in our original home.

Several years later, we sold our property, and after a series of successful real estate deals, we were able to build a house just like the one we had viewed. Hard work, determination, diligence, and some sound business wisdom all affected the process. But I don't believe it ever would have happened if Victoria had not talked me into enlarging my vision.

The Scripture says that God wants to pour out "His far and beyond favor" (see Ephesians 2:7). God wants this to be the best time of your life. But if you are going to receive this favor, you must enlarge your vision. You can't go around thinking negative, defeated, limiting thoughts. *Well, I've gone as far as my career will allow.* Or, *I've had this problem for so long; I guess it's just a part of me.*

> God wants
> this to be the
> best time of
> your life.

To experience God's immeasurable favor, you must start expecting His blessings. You must conceive it in your heart and mind before you can receive it. If you will make room for increase in your own thinking, God will bring those things to pass. But God will not pour fresh, creative ideas and blessings into old attitudes.

Centuries ago, wine was stored in leather wineskins rather than bottles. But new wine always required new wineskins, since the leather lost its elasticity as it aged. If a person poured new wine into an old wineskin, the effervescence of the new wine would cause the container to burst and the wine would be lost.

When Jesus wanted to encourage His followers to enlarge their visions, He cautioned them, "You can't put new wine into old wineskins" (see Matthew 9:17). Jesus was saying that you cannot have a larger life with restricted attitudes. That lesson is still relevant today. The good news is, God wants to fill your life with "new wine," and He wants to give you new "wineskins," new concepts, in which to contain it. But you must be willing to get rid of your old wineskins. Start thinking bigger. Enlarge your vision and get rid of the old negative mind-set that holds you back.

God says, "See, I am doing a new thing! . . . Do you not perceive it?" (Isaiah 43:19 NIV). Today, God is ready to do a new thing in your life. It pleases Him to promote you; He wants to increase you, and to give you more. But notice, God asked the question "Do you not perceive it?" In other words, are you making room for it in your own thinking? Are you believing for increase? Are you planning to excel at your job? Are you believing to be a more effective leader or a better parent?

It's time to enlarge your vision.

✷ Today's Prayer for Your Best Life Now ✷

Father, I am ready and willing to start believing You for more good things in my life. Help me get rid of those old attitudes that would limit my vision and cause Your work to be stifled in me. I will believe for better!

PROGRAM YOUR MIND FOR SUCCESS

SCRIPTURE READING FOR YOUR BEST LIFE NOW   Mark 8:31–38

Set your mind on the things above, not on the things that are on earth.

COLOSSIANS 3:2 NASB

PROGRAMMING YOUR MIND for success doesn't happen automatically. Each day, you must choose to expect good things to happen to you. When you get up in the morning, the first thing you should do is set your mind in the right direction. Say something such as "This is going to be a great day. God is directing my steps. His favor is surrounding me. Goodness and mercy are following me. I'm excited about today!" Start your day with faith and expectancy, and then go out anticipating good things. Expect circumstances to change in your favor. Expect people to go out of their way to help you. Expect to be at the right place at the right time.

Perhaps you are scheduled to give an important presentation, and you are really hoping to snag that big contract. Don't be surprised if you hear a voice whispering in your mind, *You don't have a chance. This is going to be a lousy day for you. Nothing good ever happens to you. You might as well not even get your hopes up.*

Don't listen to such lies! God *wants* you to get your hopes up. The Bible says, "Faith is the substance of things hoped for" (Hebrews 11:1 NKJV), and one definition of that sort of hope is "confident expectancy." We can confidently expect the favor of God.

Start anticipating doors of opportunity to open for you. Expect to excel in your career. Count on rising above life's challenges.

God usually meets us at our level of expectancy. That's why, in many ways, your expectations will set the boundaries for your life. Jesus said, "According to your faith . . . be it done to you." One translation puts it simply, "Become what you believe" (Matthew 9:29 THE MESSAGE).

> Your expectations will set the boundaries for your life.

Some people tend to expect the worst. Other people feel so overwhelmed by their troubles, they have difficulty believing that anything good could happen to them. You hear them saying things such as "Oh, I've got so many problems. My business is in trouble. My health is going downhill. How do you expect me to get up and say this is going to be a good day, when I have this big mess on my hands?"

Friend, that's what faith is all about. Start believing that good things are coming your way, and they will!

What are you expecting in life? Are you anticipating good things or bad things, significance or mediocrity? Don't allow your circumstances or feelings to dull your enthusiasm for life and imprison you in a negative frame of mind. Starting today, expect things to change in your favor. Expect to experience the goodness of God!

❧ Today's Prayer for Your Best Life Now ❧

Thank You, Father, that You want me to get my hopes up, that You want me to start expecting good things to happen in my life, rather than worrying about what evil might come upon me. Where my faith is weak, please help me to grow stronger so I can trust You for more and have what my faith expects.

SEEING WITH YOUR SPIRITUAL EYES

SCRIPTURE READING FOR YOUR BEST LIFE NOW   2 Kings 2:8–15

Blessed are your eyes, because they see; and your ears, because they hear.

MATTHEW 13:16 NASB

In MY BOOK *Your Best Life Now*, I tell the story of Brian, a man in his late forties who felt as though everything in his world was falling apart. One day, a friend who cared enough to level with Brian told him, "I love ya, buddy, but you need to quit focusing on all the negative; stop looking at everything you've lost and start looking at all you have left." Brian's friend challenged him, "Start believing that things are going to change for the better, not because you deserve it, but simply because God loves you that much!"

The friend's words resonated with Brian, and he took the advice to heart. By incorporating some of the key principles I shared in *Your Best Life Now*, he established fresh patterns in his life. Brian reprogrammed his mind, breaking those old negative habits and developing an attitude of faith.

Within a matter of months, his situation began to turn around. He stopped focusing on what he didn't have, on what he had lost, on his past mistakes and failures. Instead, he started dwelling on the goodness of God. He filled his mind with thoughts of hope, faith, and victory. He developed a fresh vision, expecting things to change for the better. And sure enough, that's what happened!

Remember, your actions will follow your expectations. Low expectations will trap you in mediocrity; high expectations will motivate you and propel you to move forward in life. But raising your level of expectation is not a passive process. You must actively think positive thoughts of victory, thoughts of abundance, thoughts of favor, thoughts of hope; good, pure, excellent thoughts.

The Old Testament prophet Elijah experienced numerous miracles, and his understudy, Elisha, witnessed many of them. As Elijah neared the end of his life, he asked Elisha what he would like to have from his mentor.

"I want a double portion of your spirit," Elisha replied boldly.

Interestingly, Elijah didn't rebuke his underling. He simply responded to Elisha, "You have asked a hard thing. Nevertheless, if you see me when I am taken from you, it shall be so for you; but if not, it shall not be so" (2 Kings 2:10 NASB). In a literal sense, Elijah was telling Elisha, "If God allows you to see it, you can count on your request being granted"; but we can't help but wonder if Elijah was also saying, "If you can *see* it, then you can *be* it. If you can visualize it in your heart and mind, seeing it through the screen of God's Word with your 'spiritual eyes,' it can become a reality in your life."

God is extremely interested in what you see through your "spiritual eyes." If you have a vision of victory for your life, you can rise to a new level. But as long as you have your head down, with your gaze on the ground instead of on God, you run the risk of moving

We move toward what we see in our minds.

in the wrong direction and missing out on the great things God wants to do in and through you. It's a spiritual principle as well as a psychological fact: We move toward what we see in our minds.

What do you see when you look into your future? Do you see

yourself getting stronger, healthier, and happier? Is your life filled with God's blessings, favor, and victory? You must begin to see it, if you truly hope for it to come to pass.

❧ Today's Prayer for Your Best Life Now ❧

Lord, please help me to see with my "spiritual" eyes, seeing not merely those things that currently exist, but those things that can become realities in my life.

LOOKING BEYOND WHERE YOU ARE

SCRIPTURE READING FOR YOUR BEST LIFE NOW   Philippians 3:7–14

I can do all things through Him who strengthens me.
PHILIPPIANS 4:13 NASB

MANY PEOPLE MISS pivotal opportunities in their lives because they've grown accustomed to the status quo. They expect nothing better. They refuse to make room in their own thinking for the new things God wants to do in their lives. When a great opportunity comes along, rather than latching onto it, launching out in faith, and believing for the best, they say, "Well, that could never happen to me. That's just too good to be true."

You may be thinking, *I'll just work at my same job, in this same position, for the rest of my life. After all, this is all I know how to do.*

No, quit limiting God. He may want to open a better position for you. God may intervene in your situation, causing you to be promoted. One day, you may run that entire company!

A story I told in *Your Best Life Now* illustrates how we often set our sights too low. In the story, a frog was born at the bottom of a small, circular well. He and his family lived there, and he was quite content. He thought, *Life doesn't get any better than this.*

One day, he looked up and noticed the light at the top of the well. The frog became curious, wondering what was up there. He climbed the side of the well and cautiously peered over the edge.

Lo and behold, the first thing he saw was a pond. It was a thousand times bigger than the well! He ventured farther and discovered a huge lake. Eventually, the frog hopped a long way and came to the ocean. Now he realized how limited his thinking had been.

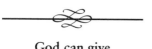

God can give you a fresh dream.

The well was a drop in the bucket compared to what God had created for him to enjoy.

Many times we're like that little frog. We've been enclosed in our own little well. It's been our comfortable environment. It's all we've ever known, a certain level of living, a certain way of thinking. All the while, God has so much more in store for us. God's dream for your life is much bigger and greater than you can imagine. If God showed you everything He had in store for you, it would boggle your mind.

Today, venture a bit further than you've gone before. Dare to dream bigger. Look out over the edge like that little frog. God has oceans He wants you to enjoy. But you've got to do your part and get outside your little box.

Many people settle for too little. "I've done as much as my education will allow me to do."

"I've gone as far in my career as I can go. I'll never make any more money than I'm making right now."

Why? Your job is not your source. God is your source, and His creativity and resources are unlimited! One idea from God can forever change the course of your life. God may give you an idea for an invention, a book, a song, or a movie. God can give you a fresh dream. He's not limited by what you have or what you don't have. God can do anything, if you believe.

Too often, we allow complacency to keep us in mediocrity. We get comfortable where we are, and we use that as an excuse. "My parents were poor," we say with a pout. "Nobody in my family has ever amounted to much, so I guess I won't either."

No, God wants you to go further than your parents ever went. He wants you to break out of that mold. Maybe you were raised in a negative environment, where everybody around you was critical, down in the dumps, and discouraged. You may be tempted to use your upbringing as an excuse to live the same way. But you can be the person to change your family tree! Don't pass that junk down to your children and keep that negative cycle going. You can be the one to break the curse in your family. You can affect future generations by the decisions you make today.

In *Your Best Life Now*, I told how my dad overcame the poorest of the poor upbringings to become the leader of one of the largest churches in America. Certainly, the odds were against him, and not surprisingly, everybody around him tried to discourage him. They said, "John, you're never going to make it out there on your own. You better stay here with us and pick cotton. That's all you know how to do. Stay here where it's safe."

But Daddy wasn't satisfied with where he was in life. He believed that God had more in store for him, and because he was willing to step out in faith, he broke that curse of poverty in our family. Now, my siblings and I, and our children, grandchildren, even our great-grandchildren, can experience more of the goodness of God because of what one man did.

You, too, can affect generations to come with the decisions that you make today. If you're not experiencing God's abundant life, let me challenge you to believe for more. Don't merely sit back and accept the status quo. Don't simply settle for what your parents had. You can go further than that. You can do more, have more, be more. Today, begin looking beyond where you are to where you want to be.

Today's Prayer for Your Best Life Now

I praise You, Father, for opening my eyes to see and understand that You have so much more in store for me. Give me the courage to believe for a good day today and a brighter tomorrow.

CHOOSE YOUR ENVIRONMENT WISELY

SCRIPTURE READING FOR YOUR BEST LIFE NOW   2 Corinthians 6:14–7:1

He who walks with the wise grows wise, but a companion of fools suffers harm.

PROVERBS 13:20 NIV

SOME FRIENDS OF mine experienced horrendous stress when they moved to a new city, and were barely able to earn enough money to pay the rent and buy food. They spent their days working hard to make a living, and pursuing new opportunities to better themselves. Obviously, they couldn't afford to spend money on entertainment. But rather than moping around their small apartment, they dressed up and went to a posh hotel, where they simply sat in the elegant hotel lobby and dreamed.

Were they wasting their time? No, they were expanding their vision, putting themselves in an environment where they could see themselves as successful. They were looking beyond where they were to where they wanted to be, and letting faith blossom in their hearts.

Perhaps you, too, need to change your environment. Quit sitting around worrying and feeling sorry for yourself. Instead, go find somewhere you can dream. It may be in a church; it may be along the banks of a stream or at a park. Find someplace where your faith will be elevated. Get into an atmosphere where people build you up rather than tear you down. Find a place where people will encourage you and challenge you to be the best you can be. Spend time with people who inspire you to reach for new heights.

If you associate with successful people, before long, their enthusiasm will be contagious and you will catch that vision. If you stay in an atmosphere of victory, you will develop a winning mind-set. If you hang around people of faith, your own faith will increase. It's time for you to soar with the eagles rather than pecking around with the chickens.

It's time for you to soar with the eagles.

Even when circumstances don't go your way, keep your mind set in the right direction. If you will do your part by continually contemplating the goodness of God, living with faith and expectancy, God will take you places you've never even dreamed of, and you'll live at a level you have never before dared to imagine.

✍ Today's Prayer for Your Best Life Now ✍

I want to live in an environment where I can dream big dreams, oh, Lord; a place where I can dare to trust You for more. Surround me, Father, with people from whom I can learn, people who will encourage me to believe Your Word. Give me the courage to take steps that will put me in contact with wise people, men and women who are considered successes in heaven.

FAMILY WITH A FUTURE

SCRIPTURE READING FOR YOUR BEST LIFE NOW   Deuteronomy 6:5–25

Truly, truly, I say to you, he who believes in Me, the works that I do, he will do also; and greater works than these he will do; because I go to the Father.

JOHN 14:12 NASB

I WAS BLESSED to be raised in a good family. I had great parents who were fine role models. My mom and dad touched people's lives all over the world. But as much as I respect what my parents have accomplished, I'm not going to be satisfied to simply inherit what they have, to do what they did. God wants each generation to go further than the previous generation. He wants each generation to be more blessed, to experience more of His love, goodness, and His influence in the world. He doesn't want you to stay where you are.

When Daddy passed away in 1999 and I took over as pastor of Lakewood Church in Houston, people often approached me and asked, "Joel, do you really think you can keep it going? You've got some real big shoes to fill."

I understood what they meant, and I appreciated their comments because they loved my dad and he was a great leader. Beyond that, few other churches the size of Lakewood had ever survived for long after the loss of the founding senior pastor, and our local press was quick to point out our low chances of success.

But none of those matters worried me. I knew God did not desire one generation to shine, and then the next generation to fade into obscurity. God wants each generation to increase.

Furthermore, I knew I didn't have to fill my dad's shoes. I had only to fill my own shoes. I just had to be the person God made me to be. When I first became the leader, people sometimes asked me, "Joel, do you think you will be able to do as much as your dad?"

I just had to be the person God made me to be.

I didn't mean it boastfully, but I always answered, "I believe I'm going to do more than my dad." That's just the way our God is. He's a progressive God. My dad brought our family from nothing to where it is today. When he started ministering, he knew little about the Bible. One of our favorite family stories was the time when Daddy first started out, he once preached an entire message on Samson, calling the hero of the story "Tarzan"!

Of course, Daddy got better and became a great preacher who influenced millions of people. Nevertheless, I say it humbly, but I believe I'm going to do far more than my dad was able to do. And I believe my children will do far more than I have done, and their children will one day do far more than all of us combined have done.

You, too, can be so much more than your predecessors, passing on a legacy of godly attitudes, blessings, and success to your children. Friend, don't ever get satisfied with where you are. Maybe you come from a family like my dad's, where they didn't have much materially. Or maybe you come from a family with tremendous wealth, prestige, and position. Regardless, you can experience more than the generation preceding you.

Maybe you hail from a long line of divorce, failure, depression, sickness, or other personal or family problems. Today is the day to say, "Enough is enough. I'm not going to pass these negative attitudes down to my children. I'm going to break that cycle and change my expectations. I'm going to start believing God for bigger and better things."

∽ Today's Prayer for Your Best Life Now ∽

Thank You, Father, that I am part of a family with a future; no longer will I be limited by my past, but I will trust You today to do things in and through my life that are even greater than the wonderful things You have done previously.

BREAKING BARRIERS

SCRIPTURE READING FOR YOUR BEST LIFE NOW   Numbers 14:5–24

*If anyone is in Christ, he is a new creature; the old
things passed away; behold, new things have come.*
2 CORINTHIANS 5:17 NASB

ONE OF THE truly inspirational stories in *Your Best Life Now* is
that of Phyllis, a woman who got pregnant when she was sixteen
years of age and dropped out of high school. Eventually, she went
on public assistance—welfare—and was barely surviving in
poverty, defeat, and despair.

But Phyllis said, "I refuse to pass this lifestyle down to my children. I'm going to make a difference with my life. I'm going to fulfill my God-given destiny. I'm going to be the person God wants
me to be." She started believing for bigger and better things, and
expecting the supernatural favor of God. She developed a "can-
do" mentality, and refused to give up.

Phyllis got a job at a school cafeteria collecting meal tickets.
The job paid minimum wage, and although Phyllis was thankful
for it, she knew God had better things in store for her. She had a
bigger dream for her life, so she went back to school and got her
high school diploma, but she didn't stop there. She worked all day
at the school and then attended college classes at night, eventually
graduating with honors. Phyllis still wasn't satisfied. She returned
to school and got her master's degree.

Today, Phyllis is not on welfare anymore; she is a principal in that same school district where she used to collect meal tickets. She did her part, and God did His.

Like Phyllis, your best days are ahead of you. God wants to do more than you can even ask or think, so don't be satisfied with past glories, and don't get stuck in the rut of past failures.

Begin believing for bigger and better things. If you don't think your dreams will ever come to pass, they never will. If you don't think you have what it takes to rise up and set that new standard, it's not going to happen. The barrier is in your mind.

That's what the Scripture calls a "stronghold" (see 2 Corinthians 10:4). It's a wrong thinking pattern that keeps us imprisoned in defeat. And that's why it is so important that we think positive thoughts of hope, faith, and victory.

Perhaps somebody has spoken negative words into your life! Maybe some so-called experts have told you that you're never going to be successful; you just don't have what it takes to make it. Reject those lies wherever you find them. After all, if God is for you, who dares to be against you? Break through those limitations and let your mind dwell on fresh, positive attitudes of faith.

Breaking those barriers will change your life and the lives of your children. Your children, grandchildren, and future generations will go further than people ever once thought possible. And it will be because you were willing to step out in faith, setting a new standard, paving the way for future generations.

On the other hand, if you fail to break through those barriers, you run the risk of spinning your wheels, going

The barrier is in your mind.

around in circles. For instance, when God led the Hebrew people out of Egypt, where they had lived in slavery for four hundred years, they headed straight toward the Promised Land. It was an eleven-day journey, but it took them forty years to get there. Because of their disobedience and lack of faith, they wandered around in the wilderness, going around the same mountain, time after time, not making any progress.

How sad! God had prepared a place of great abundance, a place of great freedom for His people. But they had been beaten down by their oppressors for so long—mistreated, used, abused, and taken advantage of—now, even though God wanted a better life for each of them, they couldn't conceive it. Rather than moving forward with an attitude of faith, expecting good things, they insisted on going around with a poor, defeated mentality. Around and around they went, focusing on their problems, always complaining, fretting about the obstacles standing between them and their destiny.

God finally jolted them out of their complacency. He said to them, "You have stayed long enough at this mountain" (Deuteronomy 1:6 NASB). I believe God is saying something similar to us. You've been wallowing where you are long enough. You can't keep going in circles, doing the same thing the same way year after year, and expect things to change. It's time to move on, to let go of past hurts, pains, or failures. It's time for increase, promotion, and favor. It's time to believe for bigger and better things.

✑ Today's Prayer for Your Best Life Now ✑

Father, I don't want to be counted among the doubters; I am a believer. I trust You to lead me in the right direction as I break through the barriers of my past. Thank You, Father, that You have good things in store, not just for me, but for my entire family!

GOD'S FAVOR IS FOR REAL

A good man will obtain favor from the LORD, *but He will condemn a man who devises evil.*

PROVERBS 12:2 NASB

ONE OF THE most important keys to living your best life now is discovering how to experience more of God's favor. The Bible states, "God has crowned us with glory and honor" (see Psalm 8:5). That word *honor* could also be translated as "favor," and *favor* means "to assist, to provide with special advantages and to receive preferential treatment." In other words, God wants to make your life easier. He wants to assist you, to promote you, to give you advantages.

But to experience more of God's favor, you must first become more "favor-minded." To be favor-minded simply means that you expect God's special help, that you are releasing your faith, believing that God wants to assist you simply on the basis that He is your heavenly Father, and He loves you.

From the time my siblings and I were little kids, every day before we left for school, our mother would pray, "Father, I thank You that Your angels have charge over my children, and that Your hand of favor will always be upon them." Consequently, I grew up with the attitude: *I'm a child of the Most High God. My Father created the whole universe. He has crowned me with favor, there-*

fore, I can expect people to go out of their way to want to help me because of my heavenly Father.

Please don't misinterpret what I'm saying. In no way should we ever be arrogant, thinking that we are better than somebody else, that everybody owes us a living or ought to bow down to us. But as God's children we can live with confidence and boldness, expecting good things. We can expect preferential treatment, not because of *who* we are, but because of *whose* we are. We can expect people to want to help us because of who our Father is.

Your Father is the King of kings, and His glory and honor spill over onto you.

I'm deeply aware that I've received tremendous favor simply because of who my earthly father was. John Osteen, my dad, was well respected and highly influential in our community. Many times people did good things for me simply because they loved my dad. One time as a teenager, I got pulled over by a policeman for speeding. But when the officer saw my license, he recognized that I was John Osteen's son. He smiled at me as though we were long-lost buddies, and he let me go with just a warning. The point is, of course, that I received preferential treatment, not because of me, but because of my father.

A correlation exists in the spiritual realm. We do not receive favor because of who or what we are. It's not because we're something special on our own merit, or that we deserve to be treated so. Nor is it because we're better than anybody else. No, you will often receive preferential treatment simply because your Father is the King of kings, and His glory and honor spill over onto you.

Nevertheless, as odd as it may sound, when you live favor-minded, declaring God's goodness, you'll be amazed at how people will go out of their way to help you. They may not even know why they're doing it, but you'll know that it is because of the favor of God.

In *Your Best Life Now*, I told of a young, successful business-man who asked me to pray with him about a job interview that represented a chance for him to advance significantly in his career. After we prayed, I encouraged him, "You have to get up every day and declare that you've got the favor of God. It doesn't matter how the situation appears, be bold and declare with confidence that you have God's favor. Throughout the day, declare, 'The favor of God is causing this company to want to hire me. The favor of God is causing me to stand out in the crowd. It's causing me to shine above the rest.'" I said, "Declare it day in and day out. Stay in an attitude of faith, and expect to get that position."

When I talked with him a few months later, he told me, "When I went in front of that board of directors, they were literally scratching their heads. They said, 'We don't really know why we're hiring you. You were not the most qualified. You were not the most experienced. You don't have the best résumé.' They said, 'There's just something about you that we like.' The board said, 'We can't quite put our finger on it. We don't know what it is, but there's something about you that makes you shine above the rest.'"

I'm convinced my friend experienced the favor of God. You can, too. You will, just as soon as you start living more favor-minded. Isn't this a great day to start expecting the favor of God to show up in the details of your life?

✥ Today's Prayer for Your Best Life Now ✥

I thank You, Father, that I have Your favor, and that I have favor with other people not because of who I am but because of who You are, and that I am Your child.

ONE TOUCH OF GOD'S FAVOR

Thou art the glory of their strength; and in thy favor our horn shall be exalted.

PSALM 89:17 KJV

I ONCE MET a mechanic who endured unfair compensation practices for years at a large diesel-truck shop where he worked. Beyond that, he endured all sorts of injustice and ridicule from his coworkers. He was one of the best mechanics in the shop, but for seven years, he didn't receive a pay raise or a bonus of any kind, basically because his supervisor didn't like him.

That mechanic could have grown bitter. He could have quit and found work elsewhere; he could have developed a chip on his shoulder and gotten mad at the world. But instead, he continued to do top-quality work, knowing that he wasn't working to please his supervisor; he was working to please God.

One day, the owner of the company called him and told him that he was ready to retire. "I'm looking for someone I can trust to take over the business and to continue the work I have started," he said. "I want to *give* it to you."

Today, the mechanic owns that company free and clear!

Friend, that is a good example of God bringing justice into that man's life. That's God paying him back, making his wrongs right. And God wants to do the same sort of thing for you.

Understand, we serve a God who wants to do more than you can ask or think. Regardless of how people are treating you, keep doing the right thing; don't get offended or upset; don't try to pay them back, returning evil for evil.

Instead, keep extending forgiveness; keep responding in love. If you do that, then when it comes time for you to be promoted, God will make sure it happens. He'll make sure you get everything you deserve, and more!

> **We serve a God who wants to do more.**

Remember, one touch from God can change your circumstances. Choose today to trust His plan for your life, and start anticipating His touch of favor.

❧ Today's Prayer for Your Best Life Now ❧

I know, Father, that one touch from You can turn around any situation in my life. I believe that You have divine favor ready to pour out in my life, and I will expect good things to come my way today because of You.

DECLARING GOD'S FAVOR

SCRIPTURE READING FOR YOUR BEST LIFE NOW   Psalm 30:1–5

The LORD is my portion; I have promised to keep Your words. I sought Your favor with all my heart; be gracious to me according to Your word.
                                            PSALM 119:57–58 NASB

DECLARING GOD'S FAVOR isn't some spooky, spiritual mumbo-jumbo. It's actually quite easy to declare God's favor in your life. Every morning, say something like this: "Father, I thank You that I have Your favor. Your favor is opening doors of opportunity and bringing success into my life. Your favor is causing people to want to help me." Then go out with confidence, expecting good things to happen, expecting doors to open for you that may not open for somebody else, knowing that you have an advantage. There's something special about you. You have the favor of God.

Anytime you get in a situation where you need favor, learn to declare it. You don't have to loudly broadcast it to the world. You can whisper it. The volume of your voice is irrelevant; it's your faith that makes the difference.

Even in the mundane aspects of life, you will not be imposing on God's goodness by declaring His favor. He wants you to act on it. For example, maybe you're stuck in traffic and you are trying to get to an important appointment. Simply declare, "Father, I thank You that I have Your favor, and that You are going to make a way for me where it appears that there is no way right now." Then keep trusting God and looking for the opportunity to open.

Perhaps you're searching for a parking spot in a crowded lot. Say, "Father, I thank You for leading me and guiding me. Your favor will cause to get me a good spot."

Keep in mind that God has your best interests at heart, that He is working everything for your good. Like a good parent, He doesn't always give you what you want. But He always gives you what you need. A delay may spare you from an accident, or cause you to bump into somebody who needs to be encouraged.

When you live favor-minded, you'll begin to see God's goodness in the everyday, ordinary details at the grocery store, at the ball field, the mall, at work, or at home. You may be at a grocery store in an extremely long checkout line, and you're in a hurry. Another checker taps you on the shoulder and says, "Come with me. I'm opening this additional register over here." That's the favor of God.

You may be out to lunch when you "just happen" to bump into somebody you've been wanting to meet. Perhaps that person is somebody you admire or hope to learn from, or possibly he or she is someone with whom you have been hoping to do business, but you couldn't get to them. That is not a co-incidence. That's the favor of God causing you to be at the right place at the right time.

> When you are living favor-minded, God's blessings seem to chase you down and overtake you.

When those kinds of things happen, be grateful. Be sure to thank God for His favor, and for His special assistance in your life. Don't take God's favor for granted. When you are living favor-minded, God's blessings seem to chase you down and overtake you. You won't be able to outrun the good things of God. Everywhere you go, things are going to change in your favor. Somebody's going to want to do something good for you, to assist you in some manner. They may not even know why. But the favor of God causes you to stand out in the crowd.

That's the sort of thing that happens "naturally" when we live favor-minded. That's why we should get in the habit of consistently speaking God's favor over our lives. And not simply over our own lives, but over our businesses, our employees, our children, and our families.

If you work in sales, you ought to declare that you have favor with your customers. Whether you are an accountant, or a lawyer, or a photographer, every day you should say, "Father, I thank You that my clients are loyal to me and want to do business with me." If you work in real estate, you ought to speak God's favor over your property: "Father, I thank You that this property is going to sell. I thank You that Your favor is leading me to the right people. Your favor is causing people to want to buy this home." Learn to speak God's favor over every area of your life. Remember, the more favor-minded you are, the more of God's favor you're going to experience.

❧ Today's Prayer for Your Best Life Now ❧

Thank You, Father, that You are opening doors for me that no one can shut. Thank You for causing people to be kind to me and to assist me. You make a way for me where it seems there is no way.

OVERTAKEN BY GOD'S GOODNESS

SCRIPTURE READING FOR YOUR BEST LIFE NOW   Genesis 6:1–9

*It is You who blesses the righteous man, O LORD; You
surround him with favor as with a shield.*

PSALM 5:12 NASB

ISRAEL'S SECOND RULER, King David was a great leader, but he
made a lot of mistakes. He committed adultery with Bathsheba
and then ordered her husband, Uriah, to be abandoned in battle,
resulting in the man's death. Nevertheless, when David repented
and sought forgiveness, God forgave him and gave him a new
start. The Bible compliments David, saying, "He was a man after
God's own heart" (see 1 Samuel 13:14; Acts 13:22). How could
that be?

David didn't focus on his faults or on the things he had done
wrong. No, when he disobeyed God or made wrong choices, he
felt remorse for those things and turned back in the right direction; he then continued to live favor-minded. It was David who
wrote, "Surely goodness and mercy shall follow me all the days of
my life" (Psalm 23:6 NKJV). Notice, he was expecting goodness
and mercy, not part of the time, but all the days of his life. I like
the way *The Message* translation puts it: "[God's] beauty and love
chase after me every day of my life." David's attitude was, "I just
can't get away from the good things of God!"

Instead of expecting to get the short end of the stick, why not start expecting God's blessings to chase after you? Instead of expecting to barely get by in life, start expecting the goodness of God to overtake you.

The favor of God can bring you out of your difficulties and turn your adversities around for good. David would say, "The favor of God keeps my enemies from triumphing over me." The Bible is replete with examples of people who were in great need, but then the favor of God came on them in a new way, providing whatever they needed.

When you are going through tough times, you must choose to be favor-minded.

The whole earth was about to be destroyed by a flood, and God gave Noah the job of building a huge boat, not to mention the gathering of the animals. No doubt, Noah was tempted to get discouraged. Yet amazingly, the Bible says, "Noah found favor in the eyes of the LORD" (Genesis 6:8 NASB). In other words, God was pleased with Noah, so the favor of God came on him in a fresh, new way, giving him unusual ability. God assisted him, and he was able to build that ark to save his family, the animals, and himself.

Consider Ruth. She was a widow living in a foreign country when the land endured a severe famine. Ruth and her mother-in-law, Naomi, were practically starving to death, so Ruth went out to the fields every day and followed behind the reapers, picking up whatever leftover grain they had missed. Ruth found favor with Boaz, the owner of the field (see Ruth 2:10), so Boaz told his workers to leave handfuls of grain on purpose for Ruth. Notice again, the favor of God came during the crisis, and before long, Ruth and Naomi's circumstances turned around, and their needs were supplied in abundance.

Joseph is another biblical example of someone who found the favor of God in adversity. He was sold into slavery in Egypt, mistreated, and taken advantage of. But the Bible says, "The favor of God was upon Joseph" (see Genesis 39:5, 21, 23). No matter what other people did to him, he continued to prosper. Even when he was unjustly accused of rape and was thrown into prison, he continued to thrive. The favor of God eventually caused him to be released, and he was put in charge of all Egypt's agricultural affairs.

In each of these examples, the favor of God came in the midst of a trial, in the midst of life's challenges. When you are going through tough times—when, like Joseph, somebody is mistreating you; or like Ruth, you're having financial difficulty; or like Noah, your whole world is falling apart—instead of becoming discouraged and developing a sour attitude, more than ever, you must choose to be favor-minded. Start today. Now is the time to allow God's goodness to overtake you. Begin declaring and expecting God's favor to show up in your life-challenges today!

⚜ Today's Prayer for Your Best Life Now ⚜

Help me, Father, to learn how to live favor-minded, to expect the best, to anticipate success rather than failure, to see good rather than evil. Even in the midst of difficulties, I will dare to believe that I have Your favor, and You will bring me out stronger, better, and more triumphant.

AN ATTITUDE OF FAITH AND FAVOR

SCRIPTURE READING FOR YOUR BEST LIFE NOW   1 Peter 1:13–25

Look forward to the special blessings that will come to you at the return of Jesus Christ.

1 PETER 1:13 NLT

HAS SOMEBODY BEEN mistreating you recently? Rather than getting angry or trying to pay them back, start saying, "Father, I thank You that Your favor is going to cause these people to start treating me well."

Similarly, if you are struggling financially, say something such as, "Father, I thank You that You're causing me to be at the right place at the right time. You are bringing wonderful financial opportunities my way."

If you will live with that sort of attitude, before long God's favor is going to show up, and that difficult situation will turn around to your benefit. The Old Testament character Job went through one of the most trying times any person could ever endure. In less than a year, he lost his family, his business, and his health. He had boils over his entire body and no doubt lived in perpetual pain. But in the midst of that dark hour, Job said, "God, I know that You have granted me favor" (see Job 10:12).

Now, here's the amazing part of the story: There are forty-two chapters in the book of Job. Job made this statement of faith in chapter 10. He was not delivered, healed, and set free until chapter 42! But at the very beginning, when his circumstances appeared darkest and most hopeless, Job looked up and declared, "God, I know You have granted me favor." Whew! That's real faith. Job was saying, "God, I don't care what the situation looks like. I don't care how badly I feel. I know You are a good God, and Your favor is going to turn this situation around."

No wonder God restored to Job twice what he had before! Friend, if you can learn to stay in an attitude of faith, and in your darkest hour boldly declare the favor of God, nothing can keep you down. The Bible says, "Hope to the end for the divine favor that is coming to you" (see 1 Peter 1:13). Certainly, this verse applies to the future blessings that Christians will receive at the return of Christ. But it is also a present truth. In other words, don't give up. Keep on believing, expecting, declaring. Keep living favor-minded, and God promises that good things will come to you. If you will keep your hope in the Lord, God says divine favor is coming. You may not be able to see it right now, but when God's favor shows up, things are going to change. Regardless of your circumstances, keep boldly declaring, "God, I know Your favor is coming my way."

"Hope to the end for the divine favor that is coming to you." 1 Peter 1:13

In *Your Best Life Now*, I shared the story of how the leaders at Lakewood Church wanted to expand our television outreach on one particular network, but the time slot we wanted wasn't available. We didn't get discouraged; we simply kept on believing for God's favor. About six months later, not only did that national network clear a space for us, they gave us a better time slot than we originally requested!

Friend, that's the favor of God.

Today, as you go about your normal activities, understand that you have His favor available to you. Live with confidence; dare to be bold. You can ask for things you normally don't ask for, and even view your adversities in a new way. Why? Because deep down inside you know you have an advantage in life. You've got an edge. You have the favor of God.

❧ Today's Prayer for Your Best Life Now ❧

Father, please help me to hope to the end, no matter what circumstances I face today, knowing that I can respond boldly and with confidence because I have Your favor. Thank You for opening doors of opportunity for me.

DREAM ON!

Scripture Reading for Your Best Life Now Daniel 1:17–21; 2:19–23

[The Lord] touched their eyes, saying, "It shall be done to you according to your faith."

Matthew 9:29 nasb

Victoria and I were in Chicago not long ago, where we met an attractive, vivacious young woman. She told us that she had lost about two hundred pounds.

"How did you do it?" I asked.

The young woman described how she had tried diet after diet but nothing seemed to work. "Then one day," she said, "I decided to start seeing myself differently on the inside. I started seeing myself losing this weight. I started seeing myself running and playing with my children. I saw myself the way I wanted to be."

She continued, "I went and I stood before that mirror and I spoke words of victory into my life. I said, 'I'm well able to lose this weight. I have discipline. I have self-control. I'm more than a conqueror.'"

What was the secret to her weight loss? She got a new image of herself; she conceived it on the inside. Once that fresh picture showed up on the inside, then God could easily develop it on the outside. Today she's living out her dream and enjoying a happier, healthier lifestyle.

I'm not saying that change will happen immediately. Nor am I saying that it's going to be easy, but I am saying that you must get an image of what you want to be on the inside first; conceive it in your heart and paint a new picture in your mind, if you want to see it come to pass in your life on the outside.

See yourself rising to new levels of effectiveness.

When I was a little boy, I often heard my father tell our church congregation, "I want you to look out there with me today and see that brand-new sanctuary." At the time, we were meeting in a small run-down building, with nothing but a parking lot full of weeds. But Daddy would say, "I want you to see that new building completed, paid off, totally debt-free." Of course, the people who were visiting with us that particular Sunday probably thought we were crazy. All they could see was a drab, brown wall. But Daddy would say, "Close your eyes and see that new church sanctuary with me through your eyes of faith. See it full of people worshiping God." We saw that sanctuary many years before it ever came to pass. And today the sixteen-thousand-seat arena of Lakewood Church in Houston has four services each weekend, all because somebody conceived it on the inside.

Think of it this way: When we close our eyes, we should see more than we do when we have our eyes open. Be a big dreamer. Don't make little plans. See your whole family serving God. See yourself rising to new levels of effectiveness.

I don't see myself at the same place next year as I am right now. I see myself reaching more people with a message of hope. I see myself as a bigger giver. I see my family healthy and happy. Sometimes I tease Victoria that I even see myself getting better looking! I see you being promoted. I see you paying off that house. I see God using you in a greater way. I see you stronger, healthier, and living a more abundant life. "How do you see all that, Joel?" you might ask. I can see it through the eyes of faith.

When I look with faith into the future for my family, I see our children marrying good people. I see our children working with us in the ministry. I see our children as the next leaders of their generation. I see our children doing great things for God.

Take a few minutes every day to dream big dreams; close your eyes, and envision your dreams coming to pass. Envision yourself out of debt. Envision yourself breaking that addiction. Envision your marriage being more fulfilled. Envision yourself rising to new levels in your career. If you can establish that picture in your heart and mind, then God can begin to bring it to pass in your life.

⟨ Today's Prayer for Your Best Life Now ⟩

Father, because of You, I will dare to dream big dreams. With faith and confidence in You, I know that I can accomplish the goals that You have placed within my heart.

PART TWO

DEVELOP A HEALTHY SELF-IMAGE

SEE YOURSELF AS GOD SEES YOU

SCRIPTURE READING FOR YOUR BEST LIFE NOW   Judges 6:11–16

The LORD is with you, O valiant warrior.

JUDGES 6:12 NASB

How you see yourself and how you feel about yourself will have a tremendous impact on how far you go in life and whether or not you fulfill your destiny. The reason your self-concept is so important is that you will probably speak, act, and react as the person you *think* you are. Psychologists have proved that you will most consistently perform in a manner that is in harmony with the image you have of yourself. If you see yourself as unqualified, unattractive, inferior, or inadequate, you will probably act in accordance with your thoughts.

Every person has an image of himself or herself. The question is, does your image of who you are line up correctly with who God says you are? Individuals who view themselves as God sees them are usually happy about who they are. They know that they have been created in God's image and He has crowned them with tremendous honor (see Genesis 1:26–27; Psalm 8:4–5). They feel good about themselves, because they know that God loves them and He feels good about them! They can honestly say, "Thank You, Father, for creating me the way You did. I know that You have a purpose and a plan for me, and I'd rather be me than any other person on earth. You have promised that You have good things in store for me, and I can't wait to discover them!"

God wants you to see yourself as a priceless treasure. He wants you to feel good about yourself. God knows you're not perfect, that you have faults and weaknesses and you sometimes make mistakes. But God loves you anyway. He created you in His image, and He is continually shaping you, conforming you to His character, helping you to become even more like Him. That's why it's important that you learn to love yourself, faults and all, not because of pride or egotism, but because that is how your heavenly Father loves you. You can hold your head up high and walk with confidence knowing that God loves you unconditionally. His love for you is based on what you are, not on what you do.

Learn to love yourself how your heavenly Father loves you.

God believes in you even more than you believe in yourself. So often, we sense God telling us that He has something big for us to do. But we say, "Oh, God, I can't do that. I'm just a nobody. I don't have what it takes."

That's how a fellow named Gideon responded in Bible times. An angel appeared to Gideon and said, "The LORD is with you, you mighty man of valor!" (Judges 6:12 NKJV). (The Amplified Bible says, "You mighty man of [fearless] courage.")

God probably said those great things to Gideon because he was secure and confident, because he was a great leader. Right? Not so. When the angel went on to tell Gideon how God wanted him to save the people of Israel from the Midianites, a vicious, pagan people who had overrun their land, Gideon showed his true colors. He replied, "How do you expect me to save the people of Israel? I come from the poorest family in all of Manasseh. And I am the least one in my father's house."

But it's interesting to note the difference between the way Gideon saw himself and the way God regarded him. Although Gideon felt unqualified, full of fear, and lacking in confidence, God still addressed him as a mighty man of fearless courage. Gideon felt weak; God saw him as strong. Gideon felt unqualified; God saw him as competent to do the job. Gideon felt insecure; God saw him with enough confidence and boldness to lead His people into battle and come out with the victory. And Gideon did!

God sees you as a champion, too. You may not see yourself that way, but that doesn't change God's image of you one bit. God still sees you exactly as His Word describes you. You may feel unqualified, insecure, or overwhelmed by life; you may feel weak, fearful, and insignificant, but today dare to start seeing yourself as God sees you—as a victor!

✑ Today's Prayer for Your Best Life Now ✑

Love myself? Those words don't come easily for me, Father. But with all my heart, I want to learn how to love myself, not so I can bask in self-adulation, but so I can more deeply appreciate who You have made me to be, and that I might more effectively express Your love to others.

IT'S OKAY TO LIKE YOURSELF

SCRIPTURE READING FOR YOUR BEST LIFE NOW   Psalm 139:1–24

Keep me as the apple of the eye; hide me in the shadow of Your wings.

PSALM 17:8 NASB

GOD WANTS YOU to feel good about yourself. He knows you're not perfect and you're going to make some mistakes, but God is not focusing on your weaknesses or what you've done wrong. God is looking at what you're doing right. He may not be pleased with every decision you have made, but understand this extremely important truth: God is pleased with you.

As long as we keep pressing forward, trying to do our best, we can hold our heads up high, knowing that God is changing us from glory to glory. Granted, at times your life may seem far from glorious. You may have some problem areas you need to overcome. Perhaps you have some bad habits yet to break, but that's okay. You don't have to go around beating yourself up, living in guilt and condemnation. No, God is in the process of changing you. But if you're constantly at strife within yourself because you feel that you aren't "good enough," your spiritual progress will be thwarted.

You must learn to accept yourself, right where you are, faults and all. You may have a problem with your temper, or some other bad habit, or maybe you're not the parent you know you should be, but if you're always rejecting yourself, living with a heaviness, thinking about what you're not, that's going to keep you from going forward to become all God wants you to be. You have to learn to accept yourself.

After all, not one of us is perfect. We all have areas in which we need to improve. Don't make the mistake of always feeling bad about yourself.

Sadly, many people don't really like themselves. They have a war raging within. They are constantly thinking or speaking negatively about themselves. They feel guilty, inferior, insecure, and condemned. Because of their own self-rejection, they can't get along with other people.

We must learn to accept ourselves, faults and all, if we want to go to a higher level. We have to come to grips with the fact that we're going to have some weaknesses. We will always have some imperfections throughout our lives. We need to give ourselves a break, and not be so hard and critical on ourselves when we don't live up to our own unrealistic expectations.

"But I can't control my temper," you may say. Or, "I've tried and tried to quit smoking and have failed time after time. I'm so undisciplined. I keep making the same mistakes. I'm sure God is just shaking His head in dismay at me."

You are not surprising God. God made you. He knows everything about you, good and bad, and God still loves you. You might as well lighten up a little and learn to love yourself. It's okay to enjoy where you are while God is in the process of changing you and taking you to where He wants you to be.

You don't have to beat yourself up all the time until you get over that bad habit. The truth is, even after you overcome that habit, God will bring another area to light with which you will need to deal. You are a work in progress, and He is constantly changing you for the better. If you don't keep a good attitude and accept yourself, faults and all, then you'll go through your entire life feeling wrong on the inside. It will affect how you see yourself—your self-image. Your relationships with other people will be affected. Most important of all, your relationship with God will be affected.

I'm not saying that it's okay to have a loose attitude toward our mistakes. Nor do we have any excuses for living sloppy lives. I'm referring to people who have a heart to do what is right, people who are trying to do their best. If that's you, then don't be condemned and live with a heavy heart, just because you have some areas you still struggle in, some areas in which God is still refining you.

God has already approved and accepted you.

You need to know God is pleased with you. You are the apple of His eye. Just as the pupil is in the center of your eye, you are the center of God's attention. You didn't choose God; He chose you. Before you were ever formed in your mother's womb, God saw you. And the Scripture teaches that God has already approved and accepted you.

If God approves you, why don't you accept and approve yourself? The Scripture doesn't say that God approves you as long as you don't make any mistakes, as long as you don't have any weaknesses. No, God approves you unconditionally. He accepts you and loves you in spite of your faults.

Sometimes I say or do things I wish I wouldn't. Sometimes I have a bad attitude. I may be selfish. But I've learned to ask God's forgiveness for my failures, mistakes, and sins, and move on. I'm not going to go around beating myself up because I'm not perfect. God knows my heart. He knows that at least I'm trying. I've made a decision to hold my head up high and feel good about myself, knowing that God approves of me. God accepts me. I know that God is pleased with me.

"Well, Joel," I hear you saying, "that sounds like a haughty attitude to me. Don't you know we're just poor old sinners?"

No, I know we *used* to be poor old sinners, but when we came to God, He washed away our sins (see 1 Corinthians 6:9–11). He made us new creatures. The Bible says, "The old things passed away; behold, new things have come" (2 Corinthians 5:17 NASB). He made us the righteousness of God. Now, we are no longer poor old sinners. We are sons and daughters of the Most High God.

Instead of having that poor-old-me mentality, expecting a crumb here and a crumb there, why don't you step up to the dinner table? God has a beautiful banquet in store for you. He has an abundant life for you. You are not a weak worm of the dust. You have royal blood flowing through your veins. Your heavenly Father created the whole universe with you in mind.

☙ Today's Prayer for Your Best Life Now ❧

Father, sometimes I have a hard time seeing myself the way You see me, so please remind me occasionally through Your Word, or through messages in everyday life. Thank You for making me special, and for not giving up on me when I make mistakes or wrong choices. Please keep changing me, making me better, more like You.

YOU ARE WELL ABLE!

[The Lord said,] "My gracious favor is all you need. My power works best in your weakness." So now I am glad to boast about my weaknesses, so that the power of Christ may work through me.

2 CORINTHIANS 12:9 NLT

ARE YOU ALLOWING your weaknesses and insecurities to keep you from being your best? Are you making excuses as to why you can't take a new leadership position at work, or get involved in some program in your church, serve in your community, or help a friend in need? Rather than giving too much attention to your insecurities and weaknesses, decide today to focus on your God.

God loves to use ordinary people just like you and me to do extraordinary things. You may not feel capable in your own strength, but that's okay. The apostle Paul said, "When we are weak, He is strong" (see 2 Corinthians 12:9–10). God is not pleased when we mope around with a "poor me" attitude and a "weak worm of the dust" mentality. When you do that, you're allowing your self-image to be shaped by nonbiblical concepts that are contrary to God's opinion of you.

Yet many people do just that. Consequently, they feel insignificant and unworthy to receive God's attention, much less His blessings. Their poor self-image keeps them from exercising their

God-given gifts and authority, and it robs them of experiencing the abundant life their heavenly Father wants them to have. Most often, the lack of joy and meaning in their lives is a direct result of how those individuals see themselves.

Beware of associating with or adopting the attitudes of people who, through their negative outlook and lack of self-esteem, will rob you of the greatness that God has for you. A classic illustration of this is recorded in the Old Testament, in Numbers 13 and 14. After God supernaturally helped Moses deliver the Hebrew people out of Egyptian slavery, they traveled to the border of Canaan, the land flowing with milk and honey. They camped right next door to the Promised Land, the place where God had promised His people they would prosper and have a fantastic future. But they would have to fight for it.

Moses sent twelve spies into Canaan to check out the opposition and get a feel for the land before launching the battle. When the spies returned with their report, they were divided in their opinion. Ten of the twelve spies said, "It is indeed a land flowing with milk and honey, but we don't have a chance. We'll never defeat those people. They're too big and they're too strong." They went on to say, "Moses, we were in our own sights as grasshoppers." In other words, compared to the opposition and the obstacles in front of them, the mental image they had of themselves was as small, weak, defeated grasshoppers, ready to be squashed, helpless before the giants opposing them.

Do you see yourself as successful?

The other two spies, Joshua and Caleb, disagreed with the majority report. "Moses, we are well able to possess the land," they said. "Yes, there are giants there, and the giants are formidable, but our God is much bigger. Granted, the people are strong, but our God is stronger. Because of Him, we are well able. Let's go in at once and possess the land."

How do you see yourself? Do you see yourself as successful? Healthy? Upbeat? Happy? Do you see yourself as being used by God? Do you see yourself as "well able" to do what God wants you to do, strong in the Lord and the power of His might? Or, have you allowed yourself to adopt a "grasshopper mentality"?

The grasshopper mentality says, "I'll never make it in life. My dreams will never come to pass. My marriage is too far gone; I'm too far in debt. I'll never get out of the hole I'm in."

God sees us as "well able" people. Not because *we* are so powerful, but because our God is so powerful! When you face adversity and hardships in life, you can rise up with boldness and confidence, knowing that because of God, you are well able to overcome them.

Learn to see yourself as God sees you—as a winner, an overcomer, as "well able." God wants you to accomplish great things in life, and He's put incredible potential, gifts, and talents within you to enable you to do so. Start stepping out in faith and acting on the desires that He's placed in your heart.

✧ Today's Prayer for Your Best Life Now ✧

I acknowledge my weakness, Father, knowing that as I trust You to work in and through me, You make me strong. You make me adequate despite my insecurities; You provide the power to accomplish all that You ask me to do.

PUT ON GOD'S APPROVAL

Stand firm then, with the belt of truth buckled around your waist, with the breastplate of righteousness in place, and with your feet fitted with the readiness that comes from the gospel of peace.

EPHESIANS 6:14–15 NIV

IN *THE LIVING BIBLE*, Ephesians 6:14 says, "You will need the breastplate of God's approval." Every morning, no matter how you feel, no matter what you may have done wrong the day before, you can get up and say, "Father, I thank You that You approve me, and that You are pleased with me. I thank You that I'm forgiven. I know that I am a friend of God."

If you'll do that, you'll be amazed at what begins to happen. Your whole self-image will change. That heavy load of guilt and condemnation will be lifted off you. You'll get your joy back. You'll go out to meet the day with a whole new attitude.

But putting on the breastplate of God's approval does not happen automatically; it is something we must do. Just as we put on our clothes every morning, we need to get up and consciously put on God's approval.

One of the worst mistakes we can make is to go through life disapproving of ourselves. Nothing will plunge you into defeat any quicker than being negative and critical toward yourself. "I don't know why I can't do anything right." "Why can't I get over this habit?" "Why am I so slow?"

The Bible says, "The righteous are bold as a lion" (Proverbs 28:1 NASB). You can't let that black cloud follow you around. You've got to rise up and do something about it. You may have a long way to go today. You may be dealing with a lot of faults. But remember, God is still working on you. You are not a finished product. You may not be all you want to be, but at least you can thank God you're not what you used to be. Stop looking at how far you have to go, and take a look at how far you've already come. Shake off that sense of unworthiness, and put on the breastplate of God's approval.

God sees your potential. He sees the person you are capable of becoming. He's not focused on what you are today; He's focused on your possibilities and what you can become. To God, you are a diamond in the rough. You may need a lot of polishing; you may have a lot of rough edges. That's okay; we all do. But God sees what's in you, and He's never going to give up on you. He will keep working on you and making you into the person He wants you to be. Jesus once said to Simon, "You are Simon, but you shall be Peter." Jesus meant, "When I get through with you, you're going to be something much greater."

When Jesus first called Simon, he had a lot of weaknesses to overcome. Simon was presumptuous, opinionated, hotheaded, self-centered, and sometimes used profane language. Why did God choose him? Why didn't God choose somebody more qualified, with fewer weaknesses?

Because God looks at the heart. Man looks on the outside, but God looks deep down into a person, and He saw what Peter could become. He looked in him and saw the possibilities. In the same way, God is not merely looking at what you are right now. He's looking at what you can become. Just like Peter, God has put more in you than you can even imagine. You have gifts and talents that nobody else has. God has planted seeds of greatness in you. Why don't you quit looking at what you can't do and start looking at what God can do? It's not where you are that matters; it's where God can take you.

The Scripture says, "Be confident of this. He that began a good work in you will continue to perform it until it's perfectly complete" (see Philippians 1:6). God is never going to quit working on us. He's not going to get halfway through and say, "I am tired of dealing with you." "You keep making that same mistake." "You've got so many faults, I've had it with you." No, God is going to keep working on us until He shapes us into the people He wants us to be.

Stay focused
on what you
can become,
and God will
get you to
where you
need to be.

But you have to do your part. Quit overanalyzing your faults; stop taking an inventory of everything wrong with you; quit keeping a running record of all your mistakes. If you make mistakes, ask for forgiveness and then move on. Don't wallow in guilt and condemnation, and don't become overly concerned if you are not changing as quickly as you would like. Your job is to keep pressing forward and doing your best. Stay focused on what you can become, and God will get you to where you need to be.

One day the famous artist Michelangelo was standing in front of a huge, unsightly piece of rock. With his hammer and chisel, he was working on the rock, in the beginning stages of sculpting it into a piece of art. He knew it was going to be a long, drawn-out process.

Somebody came along and said, "What are you doing wasting your time working on that ugly piece of rock?"

Michelangelo said, "I see a beautiful angel trapped in this rock, and I'm doing my best to let him out."

The master artist saw something that other people couldn't see. And that's exactly the way God sees us. You may have made a lot of mistakes with your life. Perhaps you've failed God a thousand times. Now, you feel that you don't deserve anything good. You may feel that you are nothing more than a useless lump of rock. But when God looks at you, He doesn't see the rock. He sees the angel trapped inside. God sees a valuable son or daughter whom He created in His own image. He's not done working on you yet. He's chipping away, knocking off the rough, unsightly edges, molding you, shaping you, until He gets the angel out of the rock.

Quit beating yourself up, thinking you've made too many mistakes. God is a God of second chances—and third, and fourth, and even more chances. He loves you. He approves of you, and God's approval is something He put in you before the foundation of the world. It is not based on your achievements or performance. It is based solely on the fact that you are His child and He sees the best in you. God accepts you. God approves you. There's nothing you can do and there's nothing anybody else can do that will ever change your value in God's eyes.

❧ Today's Prayer for Your Best Life Now ❧

Father, I thank You that You have already accepted and approved me. I may not be perfect, but You know at least I'm trying, and I'm going to go out today with my head held high, knowing that You are in the process of changing me.

GOD SEES YOUR GOOD MOVES

SCRIPTURE READING FOR YOUR BEST LIFE NOW   1 John 3:1–24

We are God's workmanship, created in Christ Jesus to do good works, which God prepared in advance for us to do.

EPHESIANS 2:10 NIV

YOUR HEAVENLY FATHER does not dwell on the times you get knocked down. He's not dwelling on your faults. No, God focuses on the things you're doing right; He sees the best in you. God sees your good moves.

You may not always control your temper as you know you should. You may disobey God's Word, or slip and say things you wish you hadn't said. Seek forgiveness from God and from anyone you may have offended, but don't go around beating yourself up, living in condemnation. As long as you are pressing forward, you can hold your head up high, knowing that you are a "work in progress," and God is in the process of changing you.

Please don't misunderstand. God does not condone wrongdoing, and we shouldn't either. But don't become so focused on your faults that you can't enjoy who God made you to be. You've got to be happy with who you are right now and accept yourself, faults and all.

Your sense of value isn't based on your achievements, how well you perform, how somebody else treats you, or how popular or successful you are. Your sense of value extends from the fact that you are a child of the Most High God. As His unique creation, you have something to offer this world that nobody else has, that nobody else can be.

You have something to offer this world that nobody else has.

It's vital that you accept yourself and learn to be happy with who God made you to be. If you want to truly enjoy your life, you must be at peace with yourself. Many people constantly feel badly about themselves. They are overly critical of themselves, living with all sorts of self-imposed guilt and condemnation. No wonder they're not happy; they have a war going on inside. And if you can't get along with yourself, you will never get along with other people. The place to start is by being happy with who God made you to be.

You may not be perfect—nobody is! Sure, you've got some flaws—we all do! Every person has weaknesses. Even the great men and women of the Bible made mistakes. They all had shortcomings, but that didn't stop God from loving them, blessing them, and using them to accomplish great deeds. To be truly free, you must have a healthy respect for yourself in spite of your "imperfections."

Don't be so hard on yourself. There may be some things in your life that you aren't happy about; you may have some habits you need to break. But remember, God is not finished with you. He's in the process of changing you.

The Scripture says we are God's workmanship (see Ephesians 2:10). The word *workmanship* implies that you are not yet a finished product; you are a "work in process." Throughout our lives, God is continually shaping and molding us. The key to future success is to not be discouraged about your past or present while you are in the process of being "completed." The Bible indicates that we go from glory to glory as we are being transformed into God's image (see 2 Corinthians 3:18). Whether you realize it or not, right now God is moving you onward toward greater things. The path of the righteous gets brighter and brighter (see Proverbs 4:18).

As you go through your day, when you are tempted to get discouraged, remind yourself that according to God's Word, your future is getting brighter; you are on your way to a new level of glory. You may think you've got a long way to go, but you need to look back at how far you've already come. You may not be everything you want to be, but thank God that you're not what you used to be.

❧ Today's Prayer for Your Best Life Now ❧

It's amazing, O God, that although You know me better than anyone, You continue to love me, faults and all. I know I can't earn Your love, Father, so let me learn to enjoy it, to embrace it, and reflect it to others.

DON'T GIVE UP ON YOURSELF

Even if my father and mother abandon me, the LORD will hold me close.

PSALM 27:10 NLT

SOME PEOPLE SEEM obsessed with putting others down; they talk negatively about you or someone you love, or something you are passionate about. You can't always ignore negative input, but don't let other people, systems, or circumstances influence your estimation of your value.

Unfortunately, you may have gone through some traumatic, painful experiences in which somebody mistreated you, used you, or rejected you. Maybe your husband or wife walked out on you and you went through a bitter divorce. Maybe a good friend turned on you for no reason, and you now feel alone and worthless. Or, maybe you felt rejected as a child, and you are living with feelings of guilt and shame. Perhaps you've even convinced yourself that the negative things that happened in your past are all your fault, that you deserve nothing but heartache, pain, guilt, and condemnation. Friend, nothing could be farther from the truth.

I recall talking to a young man who had suffered severe rejection as a child, to the point that he was convinced he was to blame for all the heartache in his family, that he was the reason his parents were so unhappy, that he'd done something wrong, that his life was one horrible mistake.

I told him, "You cannot allow your self-esteem and your sense of value to be determined by how other people treat you. The Bible tells us that God accepts us even if everybody else in this world rejects us."

I could see a glimmer of hope reflected in his eyes, so I continued to encourage him. "The psalmist said in Psalm 27:10: 'Although my mother and my father have rejected me, the Lord will take me in and adopt me as His very own child.' God will never reject you. He always accepts you. Don't allow the rejection of other people to cause you to reject yourself."

Maybe you live or work with somebody who is always putting you down and criticizing you. Let that misinformation go in one ear and out the other. Constantly remind yourself that you are made in the image of Almighty God. Remind yourself that He has crowned you with glory and honor, that you are God's own masterpiece. Don't let other people play games with your mind, deceiving you into thinking that your value is diminished.

You may feel that your dreams have been dashed by the choices you have made or—worse yet—by the choices imposed on you by others. Maybe you feel trapped in a rut, but there's hope! God wants to restore your sense of value. David wrote, "God has lifted me out of the horrible pit, and He set my feet upon a rock and put a new song in my mouth" (see Psalm 40:2–3). God wants to put a new song in your heart; He wants to fill you with hope. He wants you to know that He loves you more than you can imagine, and He can turn your dashed dreams into something beautiful.

You are God's own masterpiece.

Hold your head up high, knowing that God is in control and He has a great plan and purpose for your life. Your life may not have turned out exactly as you'd hoped, but the Bible says that

God's ways are better and higher than our ways. No matter what you go through in life, no matter how many disappointments you suffer, you will always be the apple of God's eye. He will never give up on you, so don't give up on yourself.

⚜ Today's Prayer for Your Best Life Now ⚜

I thank You, Father, that You see not just where I am today, but the potential for where I can be tomorrow. Even if other people reject me, I know that I am accepted in heavenly places. I know that I am wholeheartedly accepted by You!

YOU RECEIVE WHAT YOU BELIEVE

It shall be done to you according to your faith.
MATTHEW 9:29 NASB

OUR EXPECTATIONS WIELD tremendous power and influence in our lives. We don't always get what we deserve in life, but we usually get no more than we expect; we receive what we believe. Unfortunately, this principle works as strongly in the negative as it does in the positive.

Many people tend to expect the worst. They expect defeat, failure, and mediocrity. And they usually get what they expect; they become what they believe.

But you can believe for good things just as easily as you can expect the worst. It is possible to believe for more, to see yourself performing at increasingly higher levels in every area of life. The key is to expect good things from God. When you encounter tough times, don't expect to stay there. Expect to come out of that trouble. When business gets a bit slow, don't assume you will go bankrupt; don't make plans for failure. Pray and expect God to bring you customers.

If you go through difficulties in your marriage, don't simply give up in frustration and say, "I should have known that this marriage was doomed from the start."

No, if you do that, your low expectations will destroy your

marriage; your own wrong thinking will bring you down. Instead, ask God for wisdom, and change what you expect. Quit expecting to fail, and start believing that you are going to succeed.

Even if the bottom falls out of your life, your attitude should be: "God, I know that You are going to use this for my good. God, I believe that You're going to bring me out stronger than ever before."

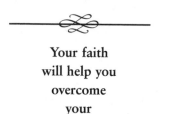

Your faith will help you overcome your obstacles.

Understand this: God will help you, but you cast the deciding vote. If you choose to stay focused on negative elements in your life, if you focus on what you can't do and what you don't have, then by your own choice you are agreeing to be defeated. You are conspiring with the enemy by opening the door and allowing destructive thoughts, words, actions, and attitudes to dominate your life.

On the other hand, if you'll get into agreement with God, if you'll focus on your possibilities, your faith can cause God to show up and work supernaturally in your life. Your faith will help you overcome your obstacles and allow you to reach new levels of victory. But it's up to you. It depends on your outlook. Are you going to focus on your problems, or will you focus on your God?

The New Testament records a fascinating account of two blind men who heard that Jesus was passing by, and faith began to rise in their hearts. They must have thought, *Maybe we don't have to stay like this. Maybe there's hope for a better future.* So they began to cry out, "Jesus, Son of David, have mercy on us and heal us" (see Matthew 9:27).

When Jesus heard their cries, He walked over to them and posed a most intriguing question. "Do you believe that I am able to do this?" He asked (Matthew 9:28 NASB). Jesus knew what they wanted; He wanted to know what they believed, whether they had genuine faith. The blind men answered back with great confidence.

They said, "Yes, Lord; we believe. We know beyond a shadow of a doubt that You can heal us. We know You are able. We have trust and confidence in You."

The Bible says, "When Jesus heard their faith, He touched their eyes and said unto them, 'According to your faith be it done unto you.' And their eyes were immediately opened" (see Matthew 9:29–30). Those men believed God could do something spectacular in their lives . . . and they received their sight!

Notice, it was their faith that turned the situation around. It was their believing that brought them the healing. Nobody can have faith for you. Other people can pray for you, they can believe for you, they can quote the Scripture to you, but you must exercise faith for yourself. If you are depending on somebody else to keep you happy, or to encourage you, or to get you out of trouble, you will live in perpetual frustration and disappointment.

Take charge of your life and decide, *No matter what comes against me, I believe in God. I'm going to have a positive outlook for my life.* What *you* believe has a much greater impact on your life than what anybody else believes.

The modern-day biblical paraphrase *The Message* relates the story about the blind men with an interesting twist: "[Jesus] touched their eyes and said, 'Become what you believe.'"

What a powerful statement! *Become what you believe!* Are you believing that God can help you to rise above your obstacles, to live in health, abundance, healing, and victory? Remember, you will become what you believe. Consider this: You are today what you believed about yourself yesterday. And you will be tomorrow what you believe about yourself right now.

∽ Today's Prayer for Your Best Life Now ∽

Father, I believe You are able to do amazing things in my life, far beyond what I can even understand. No matter what comes my way today, I will exercise my faith and believe for spectacular things that will honor You.

BE A BELIEVER

SCRIPTURE READING FOR YOUR BEST LIFE NOW 1 Thessalonians 5:12–24

I am confident of this very thing, that He who began a good work in you will perfect it until the day of Christ Jesus.

PHILIPPIANS 1:6 NASB

WHEN TIMES GET tough—as they often do—or things don't go your way—as they sometimes don't—keep on believing in God. When discouragements come or when people tell you that your dreams are never going to come to pass, you're never going to be happy, and you can never change, boldly remind yourself who is at work in your life. God is turning things around in your favor. God is opening doors of opportunity for you. He is restoring relationships; He is softening people's hearts toward you. God is completing what He started. You may not see anything happening with your natural eyes, but you must believe that in the unseen world, God is at work on your behalf.

Be a believer, but be careful what you believe. If you go around with a poor-old-me mentality, thinking that you don't deserve God's blessings, focused on your faults, always feeling badly about yourself, you will live a dismal life at best. But if you start seeing yourself as more than a conqueror, well able to succeed, strong in the Lord, the head not the tail, the victor not the victim—you will rise to a new level of fulfillment.

Dare today to start believing God for greater things. God doesn't want you to drag through life, barely making it. He doesn't want you to have to scrimp and scrape, trying to come up with enough money to pay for food, shelter, transportation, to pay your bills, or to worry about how you are going to send your children to college. He doesn't want you to be unhappy in your marriage. It is not His preference for you to live in perpetual pain.

God has a great plan for your life.

God wants you to have a good life, a life filled with love, joy, peace, and fulfillment. That doesn't mean it will always be easy, but it does mean it will always be *good*. God causes all things to work together for good to those who love Him (see Romans 8:28). You can dare to believe Him for a better marriage. Start believing Him for better health. Believe for joy and peace and happiness. Start believing for increase and abundance.

Maybe you have endured terrible disappointments. Unspeakable negative things may have happened to you, to the point that you have ceased believing for anything good to occur in your life. You've lost your dreams. You are drifting through life, taking whatever comes your way. You may be tempted to tell yourself, "I've been living this way too long. I'm never going to get any better. I've prayed, I've believed, I've done everything I know how to do. Nothing's changed. Nothing's worked. I might as well give up."

Friend, that attitude is contrary to God's desires for you. No matter how many setbacks you've suffered, God still has a great plan for your life. You *must* get your hopes up. If you don't have hope, you won't have faith. And if you don't have faith, you can't please God, and you won't see His power revealed in your life. Keep hope alive in your heart. Never give up on your dreams.

Don't allow discouragement or other setbacks to keep you from believing what God says about you.

You are never too far gone with God. Some people say, "It's too late. My life is in too big of a mess; you can't unscramble eggs," and that is true. But God can take scrambled eggs and make an amazing omelet.

✑ Today's Prayer for Your Best Life Now ✑

Father, I choose to be a believer rather than a doubter. Today, I will live with faith, trusting You for everything I need, knowing that even when tough times come, You will see me through.

GOD WANTS GOOD THINGS
TO HAPPEN TO YOU

SCRIPTURE READING FOR YOUR BEST LIFE NOW   Genesis 17:15–18:15

What is faith? It is the confident assurance that what we hope for is going to happen. It is the evidence of things we cannot yet see.

HEBREWS 11:1 NLT

BEGIN TODAY TO believe that what you have hoped for is going to happen, that good things are on their way. Remember, "Faith is the substance of things hoped for, the evidence of things not seen" (Hebrews 11:1 NKJV). Notice, faith has to do with the unseen world. You may not be able to perceive anything positive happening in your life with your natural eyes today. In fact, everything may be falling apart—your finances, your health, your business, your relationships with your spouse, children, or friends. You may have all kinds of problems, and in the natural order, it doesn't look as though anything is turning around. But don't be discouraged. Look into that invisible world, into the supernatural world, and through your eyes of faith, see that situation turning around. See your joy and peace being restored.

The world tells you, "You need to see it to believe it." But God says just the opposite. Only as you believe it will you ever see it. You've got to look through your eyes of faith and see it. Once you see it by faith, it can come into existence in the physical world.

Do you see things getting better in your life? Or are you just drifting along, accepting whatever comes your way? "I knew I wasn't going to get that promotion. Nothing good ever happens to me." "This is just my lot in life. I knew I'd never get married." "I knew I'd never be blessed."

Friend, don't limit God with your small thinking. Have a big vision for your life. Dream bigger dreams. Live with faith and expectancy. You will become what you believe.

In Part One, I referred to the Old Testament account of when God told Abraham that he and his wife, Sarah, were going to have a child—even though they were close to one hundred years old. When Sarah heard the news, she laughed. She probably said, "Abraham, you've got to be kidding. I'm not going to have a baby. I'm too old. That's never going to happen to me. And besides, look at you. You're no spring chicken either!"

And you probably recall the story: Year after year went by, and Abraham and Sarah had no children. After a while, they decided to "help" God fulfill His promise. Sarah told Abraham to sleep with her maid, Hagar. The two of them conceived, and Hagar gave birth to a child named Ishmael. But that wasn't God's best. God wanted to give Sarah a baby, one that she gave birth to herself.

Still more years went by, and no child. Finally, Sarah became pregnant. What changed?

I'm convinced that the key to the promise's coming to pass was that Sarah had to conceive it in her heart before she was able to conceive that baby in her physical body. She had to believe she could become pregnant before she actually became with child. It was nearly twenty years from the time God spoke the promise to Abraham and Sarah until the time Isaac was born. And I believe the main reason he wasn't born sooner, one of the major delays in the fulfillment of the promise for year after year, was simply the fact that Sarah couldn't see it through her eyes of faith.

Is God trying to do something out of the ordinary in your life?

Maybe the reason you have not yet seen it is because you can't conceive it. You're not in agreement with God, so you're missing out on His blessings. Jesus said, "I want you to live life to the full, till it overflows" (see John 10:10). Many times, when we read passages of Scripture such as that, the first thing we think of is why

God is trying to plant the new seed of victory inside us.

it can't happen to us. "God, I could never be healthy. I've got too many things wrong with me. I just received a bad report from the doctor." "God, I could never be prosperous. I don't have any special skill. I've never graduated from college." On and on, we tell God all the reasons why good things can't happen to us. "I'm too old. I'm too young. I'm the wrong sex. My skin is the wrong color. I'm not well educated." All that time, God is trying to plant the new seed of victory inside us. He's trying to get us to conceive. He knows if we don't conceive in our hearts through faith, it will never come to pass.

Friend, maybe God has told you something that He wants to do in your life, and in the natural, it seems totally impossible. When you look at your situation, just as Sarah looked at her physical body, you're tempted to think, *God, I don't see how You're going to bring this to pass.*

But the Bible says, "The things which are impossible with men are possible with God" (Luke 18:27 NKJV). Let that seed take root inside you. You don't have to figure out how God is going to solve your problems. You don't have to see how He's going to bring it to pass. That's His responsibility; that's not your job. Your job is to believe. Just turn that situation over to God and trust Him to take care of it. Scripture says, "God's ways are not our ways. They are higher and better than our ways" (see Isaiah 55:8). God can do what human beings cannot or will not do. He is not limited to the laws of nature. If you'll let that seed take root so it can grow, put your trust and confidence in the Lord, God will surely bring it to pass. If you can see the invisible, God will do the impossible.

⧉ Today's Prayer for Your Best Life Now ⧉

I want to get a big vision for my life, Father, and then live it out with faith and expectancy, knowing that I will become what I believe. Today, I will focus on You, who You are and what You can do in and through me.

ENOUGH CHEESE AND CRACKERS

SCRIPTURE READING FOR YOUR BEST LIFE NOW   Ephesians 3:1–21

O taste and see that the LORD is good; how blessed is the man who takes refuge in Him!

PSALM 34:8 NASB

ONE OF THE intriguing stories in my book *Your Best Life Now* is about a man who traveled across the Atlantic Ocean on a cruise ship, but never ate in the dining room with the other passengers. Instead, he would go off in a corner and eat cheese and crackers that he had brought with him on the trip. Near the end of the trip, another man asked him, "Why don't you come into the banquet hall and eat with us?"

The traveler's face flushed with embarrassment. "Well, to tell you the truth, I had only enough money to buy the ticket. I don't have any extra money to purchase fancy meals."

The other passenger raised his eyebrows in surprise. He shook his head and said, "Sir, don't you realize the meals are included in the price of the ticket? Your meals have already been paid for!"

Many people are similar to that naive traveler. They are missing out on God's best because they don't realize that the good things in life have already been paid for. They may be on their way to heaven, but they don't realize what has been included in the price of their ticket. They are surviving on cheese and crackers, while God has made much more available to them.

When we go through life with a weak worm-of-the-dust mentality, we're eating more cheese and crackers. Every time we shrink back and say, "Well, I can't do it; I don't have what it takes," we're eating more cheese and crackers. When we allow ourselves to be full of fear, worry, or anxiety, or we are uptight about something, we're over there eating more cheese and crackers.

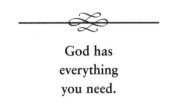

God has everything you need.

It's time to step up to God's dining table and dig in to the fabulous banquet He has prepared for you, complete with every good thing imaginable. God has everything you need—joy, forgiveness, restoration, peace, healing—anything you need to live at your full potential. It's all waiting for you at God's banquet table, if you'll pull up your chair and take the place He has prepared for you. Best of all, the price has already been paid.

You must remember that you are a child of the Most High God, and He wants you to enjoy what He has prepared for you. Just because something didn't work out your way or somebody disappointed you, that does not change who you are. Ask God today to help you develop a biblically accurate, prosperous mind-set.

And remember King David's challenge: "Taste and see that the LORD is good. Oh, the joys of those who trust in Him!"

✑ Today's Prayer for Your Best Life Now ✑

Father, I now realize that I have been existing on cheese and crackers while You have a delicious banquet prepared for me . . . and the price has already been paid! Thank You, Father, for blessing me today.

ACCORDING TO HIS RICHES

Scripture Reading for Your Best Life Now   John 2:1–11

My God will supply all your needs according to His riches in glory in Christ Jesus.

PHILIPPIANS 4:19 NASB

MY FATHER GREW up with a "poverty mentality." That's all he had ever known. When he first started out as a pastor, the church could afford to pay him only $115 a week. Daddy and Mother could hardly survive on that little amount of money, especially once my siblings and I came along. Worse yet, however, was that Daddy had come to expect poverty. For a number of years, he wasn't even able to accept a blessing when it came.

Once, a businessman in the church handed my dad a check for a thousand dollars, to help out with some unexpected expenses Daddy had incurred while serving the church. In today's dollars, that one thousand dollars would probably be equal to about ten thousand dollars!

Daddy was overwhelmed by the man's generosity, but he said, "Oh, no, brother, I could never receive this money. We must put it in the church offering."

Daddy later admitted that deep down inside, he really wanted to keep the money. He knew that he and Mother needed that money, but he had a false sense of humility. He couldn't receive the blessing. He thought he was doing God a favor by staying poor.

God was trying to bless and increase my dad. He was trying to prosper him, but because of Daddy's deeply embedded poverty mentality, he couldn't receive it. I'm so glad that Daddy later learned that as God's children, we are able to live an abundant life, that it is okay to prosper; that we should even expect to be blessed. Indeed, it is as important to learn how to receive a blessing as it is to be willing to give one.

Maybe you have come from a poor environment, or maybe you don't have a lot of material possessions right now. That's okay; God has good things ahead for you. But let me caution you: Don't allow that poverty image to become ingrained inside you. Don't grow accustomed to living with less, doing less, and being less to the point that you eventually sit back and accept it: "We've always been poor. This is the way it's got to be."

No, start looking through eyes of faith, seeing yourself rising to new levels. See yourself prospering, and keep that image in your heart and mind. You may be living in poverty at the moment, but don't ever let poverty live in you.

The Bible clearly shows that God takes pleasure in prospering His children. As His children prosper spiritually, physically, and materially, their increase brings God a sense of satisfaction that we can only imagine.

God is honored and pleased when we develop a prosperous mind-set.

What would you think if I introduced our two children to you and they had holes in their clothes, uncombed hair, no shoes, and dirt under their fingernails? You'd probably say, "That man is not a good father. He doesn't take good care of his children." Indeed, my children's poverty would be a direct reflection on me as their dad.

Similarly, when we go through life with a poverty mentality, it is not glorifying to God. It does not honor His great name. No, God is honored and pleased when we develop a prosperous mindset. God wants to supply every need you have, and He will!

≈ Today's Prayer for Your Best Life Now ≈

God, I thank You that You have better things in store for me than I would even choose for myself, that Your dream for me is even grander than my dream for myself, and Your resources are inexhaustible!

HOW LOW CAN YOU GO?

SCRIPTURE READING FOR YOUR BEST LIFE NOW   2 Samuel 9:1–13

*Whatever you ask in My name, that will I do, so that
the Father may be glorified in the Son. If you ask Me
anything in My name, I will do it.*

JOHN 14:13–14 NASB

WHAT A TRAGEDY it would be to go through life as a child of
the King in God's eyes, yet as a lowly pauper in our own eyes.
That is precisely what happened to a young man in the Old Testament by the unusual name of Mephibosheth.

Mephibosheth was the grandson of King Saul and the son of
Jonathan. Jonathan and David were best friends and had actually
entered into a covenant relationship, similar to the ancient
covenant of being "blood brothers." That means whatever one
had, it belonged to the other. Moreover, in the covenant relationship, if something were to happen to one of these two men, the remaining "brother" would be obligated to take care of the other's
family.

King Saul and Jonathan were killed in battle on the same day,
and when word got back to the palace, a servant grabbed Mephibosheth, Jonathan's little son, picked him up, and fled the city.
Going out of Jerusalem in such haste, the servant tripped and fell
while carrying the child. Mephibosheth became crippled as a result of the fall. The servant transported Jonathan's son all the way

to a city called Lodebar, one of the most poverty-stricken, desolate cities in that entire region. That is where Mephibosheth, grandson of the king, lived almost his entire life. Think about that. He was the grandson of the king, yet he was living in those terrible conditions.

Is your self-image so contrary to the way God sees you that you are missing out on God's best?

David succeeded Saul as king, and years later, long after Saul and Jonathan had passed away, David asked his staff, "Is there anyone left from the house of Saul that I could show kindness to for Jonathan's sake?" Remember, that was part of the covenant Jonathan and David had entered: If something happens to me, you will take care of my family. But by now, most of Saul's family members were dead, and thus David's question.

David was informed that Jonathan had a son that was still alive, so he ordered that the man be brought to the palace. When Mephibosheth arrived, he was no doubt fearful. After all, his grandfather had chased David throughout the country trying to kill him. Now that Saul's family had been decimated and was no longer a threat to David, Mephibosheth may have felt that David planned to execute him as well.

But David said to him, "Don't be afraid. I want to show kindness to you because of your father, Jonathan. I'm going to give you back all the land that once belonged to your grandfather Saul. And from this day forward, you will eat at my table as though you were one of my sons." David treated Mephibosheth as royalty. After all, he was the grandson of the king. And David was in a covenant relationship with his father.

Mephibosheth's life was transformed instantly—that's the good news—but think of all the years he lived in that dirty city of Lodebar. All the while, he knew he was royalty; beyond that, it was commonly known that David and Jonathan were in a covenant relationship. Based on that alone, Mephibosheth knew he had rights. He could have gone to the palace and said, "King David, I'm Jonathan's son. I'm living in poverty down in Lodebar, and I know that I'm made for more than that. I'm here to claim what belongs to me through my father's covenant relationship with you."

Why did Mephibosheth settle for mediocrity? We catch a clue from his initial response to David. When David told him that he was going to take care of him, the Bible says, "Mephibosheth bowed his head low and he said, 'Who am I that you should notice such a dead dog like me?'" (see 2 Samuel 9:8). What does this reveal about his self-image? He saw himself as defeated, as a loser, as an outcast. Yes, he was the grandson of the king, but his inner view of himself kept him from receiving the privileges that rightfully belonged to him.

Are you doing something similar? Is your self-image so contrary to the way God sees you that you are missing out on God's best? God sees you as a champion. You see yourself as a dead dog.

But just as Mephibosheth had to cast off that "dead dog mentality," replacing it with a prosperous mind-set, you and I must do something similar. You may have been hurt in life, or maybe you have made some wrong choices. But if you have honestly repented and done your best to do right since then, you no longer have to live with guilt and shame. You may not be everything you want to be. You may be crippled physically, spiritually, or emotionally. That does not change God's covenant with you. You are still a child of the Most High God. He still has great things in store for you. Be bold and claim what belongs to you.

⪘ Today's Prayer for Your Best Life Now ⪘

I know it is not because of my goodness that Your kindness is extended, O God, but because of the covenant relationship I have been blessed to inherit. Help me to better understand Your grace and Your goodness as I take my place at Your table. Thank You, Father, for making a place for me!

BE AN ORIGINAL

Don't copy the behavior and customs of this world, but let God transform you into a new person by changing the way you think. Then you will know what God wants you to do, and you will know how good and pleasing and perfect his will really is.

ROMANS 12:2 NLT

MANY SOCIAL, PHYSICAL, and emotional problems stem from the fact that people don't like themselves. They are uncomfortable with how they look, how they talk, or how they act. They don't like their personality. They are always comparing themselves with other people, wishing they were something different. "If I just had his personality . . ." "If I lived where they lived . . ." "If I looked like she looks . . ." "If my thighs just weren't so big . . ." "If I had less here and more somewhere else, then I'd be happy."

No, you can be happy with who God made you to be, and quit wishing you were something different. If God had wanted you to look like anyone else, He would have made you look like them. If God had wanted you to have a different personality, He would have given you that personality. Don't compare yourself to other people; learn to be happy with who God made you to be.

God doesn't want a bunch of clones. He likes variety, and you should not let people pressure you or make you feel badly about yourself because you don't fit their image of who you should be.

Be an original, not a copycat. Dare today to accept the person God made you to be and then go out and be the best *you* that you can be. You don't have to look or act like anyone else. God has given us all different gifts, talents, and personalities on purpose. You don't really need anybody else's approval to do what you know God wants you to do.

> Dare today
> to accept the
> person God
> made you
> to be.

Certainly, you should always be open to wise counsel. I'm not suggesting that you be foolish or rebellious. Nor am I suggesting that you move from liberty to license in your spiritual life. We never have permission to live an ungodly life. But we do have God's blessing to be confident, not letting outside pressures mold us into something or someone we're not. Be secure in who you are. If you want to join the choir at church or start a new business or buy a new car or home, you don't need anyone's approval. Your attitude should be: *I am confident in who I am. I'm not going to go around pretending, wishing I were something else, trying to fit into everybody's mold. I am free to run my own race.*

God went to great lengths to make sure that each of us is an original. We should not feel badly because our personalities, tastes, hobbies, or even spiritual proclivities are not the same as another person's. Some people are outgoing and energetic; others are more timid and laid-back. Some people like to wear suits and ties; other people are more comfortable wearing blue jeans. Some people close their eyes and lift their hands when they worship God; others worship God in a more subdued manner. And God likes it all!

Don't think that you have to fit into somebody else's mold and, similarly, don't be upset when other people don't fit into your mold. Live this day with the attitude, *I am enjoying the person God made me to be.*

∽ Today's Prayer for Your Best Life Now ∽

Thank You, Father, for making me the way I am, with all my strengths and weaknesses. Help me to enjoy being the person You created, and to live each day knowing that You have placed me on earth at this time on purpose. Thank You for giving my life meaning and significance.

RUN YOUR OWN RACE

Scripture Reading for Your Best Life Now   1 Corinthians 9:24–27

Let us run with endurance the race that is set before us, fixing our eyes on Jesus, the author and perfecter of faith.

HEBREWS 12:1–2 NASB

I ONCE HEARD a minister on television tell how he got out of bed every day at four o'clock in the morning and prayed for two hours. My first reaction was, *Oh, my. I don't pray for two hours a day, and I surely don't get up that early.* The more I thought about it, the worse I felt!

Finally, I had to say, "That's great for him, but thank God, it's not great for me! I'm going to run my race, and I'm not going to feel guilty just because I'm not doing what he's doing."

God has an individual plan for each of our lives. Just because something works for somebody else doesn't necessarily mean it's going to work for you. If we make the mistake of trying to copy other people, we're going to be frustrated, and we're going to waste a lot of time and energy. Worse yet, we may miss the good things God has for us to do.

Some mothers are always running their children here and there, investing a lot of time in their kids. Their children are involved in every club and sport, and for some folks, that's great. But some moms simply try to copy another person, or they enroll their children in all sorts of activities out of a sense of guilt and condemnation. Some frantic, frazzled parents are so desperately trying to keep up with their peers (*their* peers, not their children's), they are missing the entire point of the horizon-expanding programs in the first place. Not only that, but all that running around is wearing out Mom and Dad!

Here's some good news: You can run your own race and God will be pleased. God has given you the grace to do what He's called you to do. He has not given you the grace to do what everybody else is doing.

The Scripture teaches, "Let each one examine his own work" (Galatians 6:4 NKJV). In other words, you take care of you; quit looking at what everybody else is doing and run your own race. If you are the best that *you* can be, then you can feel good about yourself, regardless of whether you come in first or last, whether you get the big promotion or not, whether you make the grade or fall on your face in failure. If you do the best *you* can do, you can hold your head high.

Granted, you will face enormous pressure to do what everybody else is doing, to try to please everybody and meet all their expectations. If you're not careful, though, your life can become a blur, a pale imitation rather than an original. But you don't have to please everyone else; you need to please only God. The truth is, if you're going to run your own race, you may not be able to meet other people's expectations. You can't be everything to everybody. You'll have to accept the fact that some people may not like you. Everybody's not going to agree

Run your own race and God will be pleased.

with every decision you make. You probably will not be able to keep every person in your life happy. But you can't let the demands, pressures, and expectations from others stop you from doing what you know God wants you to do.

When you face difficult decisions or uncertain choices, it helps to seek counsel from someone you respect. Certainly, as the Bible says, "there's safety in a multitude of counselors" (see Proverbs 24:6), and we should never be hardheaded and stubborn. We should always stay open and be willing to take advice. But after you've prayed about something and looked at all the options, be bold enough to make a decision that is right for you. If you're trying to please everybody else by doing things you don't really want to do, so you won't hurt somebody's feelings or because you are trying to keep everybody happy, you will be cheating yourself. You can run yourself in circles trying to be something that you're not, and you'll run the risk of missing out on God's best for your own life.

Sometimes you can even get too much advice. Conflicting opinions can cause confusion. Sometimes the friends who are giving you advice can't even run their own lives. But they sure are good at telling you how to run yours! Be careful about whom you allow to influence your decision-making process. Make sure the people who are giving you advice know what they're talking about and are people who have earned your respect as a source of wisdom. Then, you need to follow your own heart in light of God's Word and do what you feel is right and good for you.

❧ Today's Prayer for Your Best Life Now ❧

Thank You, Father, for giving me the confidence to be me. Help me to run my race and to not be concerned about what other people expect of me. As long as You are pleased with me, I am happy!

YOUR TIME TO SHINE

SCRIPTURE READING FOR YOUR BEST LIFE NOW   1 John 2:12–20

Have I not commanded you? Be strong and courageous!
Do not tremble or be dismayed, for the LORD your God
is with you wherever you go.

JOSHUA 1:9 NASB

ONE OF THE things I appreciated about my mom and dad's parenting style was that they never planned my siblings' lives or my life. Certainly, they pointed us in the right direction, offering advice and wise counsel. They helped us see where our gifts and talents were, even those that were buried. But they always let us fulfill our own dreams. From the time I was a little boy, I knew my dad wanted me to preach, but I never had that desire. Despite his disappointment, Daddy didn't try to cram preaching down my throat. He didn't make me feel guilty or that I was less of a person because I wasn't doing exactly what he wanted me to do. In fact, he often told me, "Joel, I want you to fulfill your dreams for your life, not my dreams for your life." Today, I can preach with freedom because I know I'm not merely doing what pleases my family members and friends; I'm doing what pleases God.

Are you pretending to be something you're not, trying to be what everybody else wants you to be, living up to their expectations and following their dreams for your life? When my dad went to be with the Lord and I became the senior pastor at Lakewood

Church, one of my biggest concerns was "How is everybody going to accept me?" After all, Daddy had been there for forty years, and everyone was accustomed to him. His style and personality were much different from mine. My dad was a fireball of a preacher, always energetic and exciting. I'm much more laid-back.

Are you pretending to be something you're not?

One night I was praying, asking God what I should do. "Should I try to be more like my dad? Should I copy his style? Should I preach his messages?" On and on I went. I was just so concerned about it. But the Lord spoke to me, not out loud, but deep down in my heart, saying, *Joel, don't copy anybody. Just be yourself. Be who I created you to be. I don't want a duplicate of your dad. I want an original.*

That truth set me free!

When Moses died, God selected Joshua to take over as leader of His people. God said to Joshua, "Just as I have been with Moses, I will be with you" (Joshua 1:5 NASB). Notice He didn't say, "Joshua, you need to try to be just like Moses, then you'll be okay." No, God said to Joshua, "Be who I made you to be, and then you'll be successful."

One of the secrets of any success I've had at Lakewood—and I know it all comes from God—would be that I have walked in my own shoes. I haven't tried to fill Daddy's shoes or anyone else's. I have not tried to be something I'm not or tried to copy somebody else. I don't step up on the platform and act one way, then go home and act another way. No, with me, what you see is who I am. That's all God requires me to be.

And that's all He expects of you, as well. You may have some faults, some areas you and God are refining. But remember, God is in the process of changing you. And if you will choose to be happy with who God made you to be, and make a decision that today you're going to be the best you can be, God will pour out His favor in your life.

⊰⊱ Today's Prayer for Your Best Life Now ⊰⊱

Knowing that You have a tremendous plan for my life gives me confidence to use the gifts and talents You have given me, Father. I appreciate my parents and others who have sown good things in my life, but it is my time to shine, my time to fulfill my destiny, and to become all that You intend for me to be.

PART THREE

DISCOVER THE POWER OF YOUR THOUGHTS AND WORDS

THINK ABOUT WHAT YOU'RE THINKING ABOUT

SCRIPTURE READING FOR YOUR BEST LIFE NOW   Matthew 15:1–20

As he thinks within himself, so he is.

PROVERBS 23:7 NASB

MANY PEOPLE ARE not reaching their full potential because their thinking patterns are defective. You cannot think negative thoughts and expect to live a positive life. You can't think thoughts of failure and expect to succeed. Your life will follow your thoughts.

If you are constantly seeing the worst in every situation, you may not realize it, but your own thinking is drawing in more negative input. Just like a magnet, you will attract what you continually think about. You'll draw in negative friends and negative circumstances. I hear people say all the time, "I never get any breaks. Nothing good ever happens to me. I knew I wasn't going to get that promotion."

Unfortunately, they get exactly what they expect. Friend, your life is not going to change until you first change your thinking. You may be in negative circumstances today; you may have unfair things happening to you. But don't make the mistake of dwelling on those things. You've got to get your mind moving in a new direction. The Scripture says, "Set your minds and keep them set on . . . the higher things" (Colossians 3:2 AMP). That simply means set your mind on positive things. Every day, when you first get up, set your mind for success, set your mind for victory, set your mind so you can enjoy that day. If you don't set the direction for your life, if you don't choose what kind of day you're going to have, your mind will soon be filled with all sorts of negative, discouraging thoughts. *It's Monday morning, and I can't stand my job. Traffic's going to be terrible. It's my one day off and I have so much to do that I'll never get done. My back hurts. It's going to be a lousy day.*

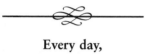

Every day, when you first get up, set your mind for success.

No, you must set your mind on the right course. Don't ever start your day in neutral. Don't wait to see what kind of day it's going to be before you decide whether you're going to be happy. Don't wait till you read the newspaper or check the weather forecast. Don't wait till you determine what sort of mood your boss is in. No, right at the beginning of your day, set your mind in a positive direction. Agree with the psalmist, "This is the day the Lord has made and I'm going to be happy. I'm going to enjoy this day. I'm going to go out and be productive. I'm going to be a blessing to somebody, and this is going to be a great day in my life."

"But Joel, you don't understand my situation," you may be saying. "My health is going downhill," or "My marriage is not what it should be," or "I'm having so many financial problems."

No, you've got to quit dwelling on all that. Don't magnify your problems. Magnify your God. The bigger we make God, the smaller our problems become. Quit dwelling on what's wrong in your life, and start dwelling on what's right in your life. Learn to focus on your possibilities, on what you can do, on your potential. Then go out each day expecting good things. Start expecting to be at the right place at the right time. Start expecting things to change in your favor. Friend, if you are going to live your best life now, you must learn how to control your thought life. Or, as I like to put it: You've got to think about what you're thinking about!

❧ Today's Prayer for Your Best Life Now ❧

I want to align my thoughts with Your Word, Father. Help me to reject any thought that would lead me away from the truth, and all that You have for me. Today, I will let my mind dwell on the good things of God.

AS YOU THINK, YOU WILL BE

Scripture Reading for Your Best Life Now   Philippians 4:4–8

Throw off your old evil nature and your former way of life, which is rotten through and through, full of lust and deception. Instead, there must be a spiritual renewal of your thoughts and attitudes.

Ephesians 4:22–23 NLT

You may not realize it, but you can choose your thoughts. Nobody can make you dwell on something. You decide what you will entertain in your mind. Your mind is similar to a giant computer in that your brain stores every thought you've ever had. That's encouraging when you're trying to find your car keys, but it's not such good news when you consider the amount of smut, foul language, ungodly concepts, and other negative input with which we are inundated every day of our lives. Nevertheless, simply because a destructive thought is stored in your mental computer does not mean you have to pull it up and run it on the main screen of your mind.

If you make that mistake and start dwelling on it, that thought will affect your emotions, your attitudes, and—if you continue to give it free rein in your mind—it will inevitably affect your actions. You will be much more prone to discouragement and depression, and if you continue pondering that negative thought, it holds the potential to sap the energy and strength right out of you.

You will lose your motivation to move forward in a positive direction.

The more we dwell on the enemy's lies, the more garbage we willingly allow him to dump into our minds. It's as though we have flung the door wide open and put up a sign that reads: "Trash goes here!"

What are you allowing your mind to dwell on? Are you constantly contemplating negative things? How you view life makes all the difference in the world—especially for you!

It's unrealistic to ignore problems and live in denial, pretending that nothing bad ever happens to us. Bad things do sometimes happen to good people, just as good things often happen to bad people. Pretense is not the answer; nor is playing semantic games to make yourself sound more spiritual. If you are sick, it's okay to admit it; but keep your thoughts on your Healer. If your body is tired, if your spirit is weary, sometimes the most spiritual thing you can do is to get some rest. But focus your thoughts on the One who has promised, "Those who wait on the LORD shall renew their strength" (Isaiah 40:31 NKJV).

Tough times come to all of us. Jesus said, "In this life you will have trouble, but be of good cheer, for I have overcome the world" (see John 16:33). He was saying that when troublesome times come, we can choose our attitudes. We can choose to believe that He is greater than our problems; we can choose the right thoughts.

We can choose to believe that He is greater than our problems.

Today, if you will dwell on the promises of God's Word, you will be filled with hope. You will develop a positive attitude of faith. Like metal filings being pulled across a desk by a magnet, you will draw in the good things of God.

A lot of people say, "Well, as soon as my situation turns

around, I'll cheer up. As soon as I get out of this mess, I'll have a better attitude."

Unfortunately, that's not going to happen. You have the process backward. You must cheer up first, then God will turn your situation around. As long as you harbor that poor, defeated outlook, you will continue to live a poor, defeated life.

Interestingly, the Scripture says, "Strip off the old nature and put on the new man." It says, "Be constantly renewed in the spirit of your mind, having a fresh mental and spiritual attitude" (see Ephesians 4:22–24). You can't sit back passively and expect this new person to suddenly appear; nor can you go through life in a negative frame of mind and expect anything to change for the better. No, you need to strip off those old negative thoughts and "put on" a fresh new attitude. In other words, you must change your thought patterns and start dwelling on the good things of God.

The first place you must win the victory is in your own mind. If you don't think you can be successful, then you never will be. If you don't think your body can be healed, it never will be. If you don't think God can turn your situation around, then He probably won't. Remember, "As a person thinks in his heart, so he will become" (see Proverbs 23:7). When you think thoughts of failure, you are destined to fail. When you think thoughts of mediocrity, you are destined to live an average life. But friend, when you align your thoughts with God's thoughts and you start dwelling on the promises of His Word, when you constantly dwell on thoughts of His victory, favor, faith, power, and strength, nothing can hold you back. Make up your mind today to think positive, excellent thoughts, and you will be propelled toward greatness, inevitably bound for increase, promotion, and God's supernatural blessings.

⧜ Today's Prayer for Your Best Life Now ⧜

Today, I choose to dwell on good thoughts, thoughts that are based on the truths of Your Word, Father; thoughts that will build me up rather than tear me down. Thank You for re-newing my mind and giving me a fresh new attitude of hope.

DON'T GIVE FEAR A THOUGHT

What I fear comes upon me, and what I dread befalls me.

Job 3:25 NASB

A few years ago, I met an extremely discouraged young couple after a church service. They wanted to have a baby, but for some reason, throughout their marriage they had not been able to conceive a child. They'd been to various doctors, and the young man and young woman both had been thoroughly examined; everything checked out okay medically. According to the doctors, there was no medical reason why she could not get pregnant. Yet they could not conceive.

The couple came to see me, and as the young woman told me their story, I noticed that she was becoming more agitated and upset. She said, "Joel, my mother had a terrible time conceiving me. My grandmother had problems with infertility, as well. Ever since I was a little girl, I've always been afraid that I might not be able to have a baby, and I love children so much. It is frustrating. I always knew that this was going to happen to me."

I said, "That could be your problem right there. You have to change your thinking. Begin to believe God for your baby. Expand your horizons and get a better vision of what is possible."

Fear had created a stronghold in that young woman's mind.

Mentally, she didn't think she could conceive; she didn't believe she could ever have her own baby, so her thinking was keeping her in bondage physically. The thing she had feared the most had come upon her.

I told her, "From this day forward, I want you to get a fresh vision of what God can do in your life. You should start seeing yourself with that child. You have to look out through your eyes of faith and see yourself holding that little baby. Throughout the day, meditate on God's Word. Go around dwelling on the fact that 'the fruit of my womb is blessed.' Remind yourself of the Scripture that says, 'No good thing will God withhold from me when I walk uprightly.' Think on the truth that children are a gift from God. Keep running those thoughts through your heart and mind. Say, 'Father, I thank You that we are blessed, that we are well able to conceive this baby.'"

The young couple left encouraged, and about six months later, she became pregnant. Nine months after that, she gave birth to a beautiful baby boy.

Her fear had created a barrier that blocked her ability to conceive. Once the couple developed a fresh vision of what God could do, they overcame the fear, and life took on an entirely new dimension.

Many people dwell on the negative and then wonder why nothing positive ever happens to them. It's because their minds are focused in the wrong direction. You can't constantly think thoughts of worry and fear and expect to have any kind of victory in your life. The Scripture tells us, "God has not given us a spirit of fear, but of power and of love and of a sound mind" (see 2 Timothy 1:7). The Amplified Bible describes a sound mind as a "well-balanced mind" and adds "discipline and self-control." In other words, to live in victory, we must discipline our minds to think thoughts that are consistent with God's Word.

Every day you will have negative thoughts bombard your mind. You can't avoid them. But you can choose whether you will give them life by dwelling on them. You can control the doorway to your mind, reject the negative thoughts, and choose to dwell on something good. The Bible says, "This book of the law shall not depart from your mouth, but you shall meditate on it day and night, . . . for then you will make your way prosperous, and then you will have success" (Joshua 1:8 NASB). Notice, God said if we'll think about His Word day and night, and fill our minds with thoughts of faith and victory, then we will have successful lives.

> Choose to dwell on something good.

To meditate means to think about the same thing over and over. What are you meditating on? What's going on in your mind? Your consistent thoughts will determine what kind of life you live. If you go around full of fear all the time, you may not realize it, but you are actually believing for the negative. You're activating the enemy's power. When you do that, don't be surprised if you don't get just what you're believing for.

The Old Testament story of Job has many lessons for us, but one especially powerful principle is revealed early in the calamities that came upon that good man. He lamented, "The thing I greatly feared came upon me. And that which I dreaded has happened" (see Job 3:25). When good people agree with the enemy, he is given the right to bring bad things into being.

Many people spew a litany of fear-filled ideas in their daily conversations. "I'm afraid my business is never going to grow." "I'm afraid my children are running with the wrong crowd," or "I'm afraid I'm going to get that same sickness my mother had. After all, it's been in our family for three generations."

No, recognize what those thoughts and comments are doing. You are giving the enemy a foothold, an open door, a free shot at you and your family. Instead, if your family has a history of ill health, put your foot down and say, "No more! This is a new day. We may have suffered with that disease in the past, but now that curse has been broken. It stops right here with me." Your attitude needs to be, *Grandmother may have died from cancer. Mother may have suffered with it. Great-grandmother may have had it. But as for me and my house, we're going to live long, healthy lives! I'm going to draw that line in the sand. Today the tide of the battle has turned.*

In my family, on my father's side, we have a long history of heart disease. My dad's dad, many of his uncles, and other relatives all died early deaths from heart disease. I could easily go through life thinking, *Well, everybody else has had high blood pressure and clogged arteries. I guess I'm going to have the same thing.*

No, I know better than that. I've made up my mind that I'm going to be healthy. I plan to pass down good health and attitudes to my children. I'm going to establish a pattern of long life. I don't have to be afraid of getting the same illnesses that somebody else had, not even those to which I may have a predisposition because of my family background or my genes.

I was talking with a middle-aged man recently who was so worried that he was going to get Alzheimer's disease. He said, "Joel, everybody in my family gets it. I've had uncles, relatives, aunts, and parents who have developed Alzheimer's, and I'm worried that I'm going to get it, too." It was almost as if he was planning on it happening, as though he was already making his reservations.

I told him, "Unless you change your thinking, you're going to get just what you're believing for."

"What do you mean?" he asked. "I'm not believing for that disease."

I said, "When we live with fear, expecting the worse, we're agreeing with the enemy, and opening the door to all the trouble he can bring us. You can either act in faith and receive God's blessings and favor, or act in fear and receive the defeat and misery from the enemy." I challenged him to set his mind in a new direction, meditating on the good things of God.

The things we fear can come upon us. Get in the habit of meditating on God's Word, and you will discover that God has a great plan for your life. You'll find that God is guiding you, that He's bigger than any of your problems, and He can turn any situation around in your favor.

Your thoughts should be, *I know something good is going to happen to me. I know God is at work in my life. I know my business is going to prosper. I know my family is going to thrive; my children are going to excel.* God wants us to dwell on thoughts of faith, victory, and hope. You could see your whole life turn around today if you'd simply start thinking the right thoughts, thoughts that are consistent with the positive principles of God's Word.

Today's Prayer for Your Best Life Now

Father, please help me to dwell on thoughts that are pleasing to You, thoughts of a great future, of my family enjoying Your good gifts and having lives characterized by usefulness, significance, and blessing.

MAINTAIN A POSITIVE MIND-SET

SCRIPTURE READING FOR YOUR BEST LIFE NOW   Colossians 3:1–17

Let this mind be in you which was also in Christ Jesus.
PHILIPPIANS 2:5 NKJV

WE MUST CONTINUALLY choose to keep our minds set on the higher things. The Bible says, "Set your minds on the things which are above" (see Colossians 3:2). Notice again that there is something we are to do—we must continually choose, day in and day out, twenty-four hours a day, to keep our minds set on the higher things. What are those things that are above, the higher things? Quite simply, they are the positive things of God. The apostle Paul provides a great list by which we can evaluate our thoughts: "Whatever things are true, whatever things are noble, whatever things are just, whatever things are pure, whatever things are lovely, whatever things are of good report, if there is any virtue and if there is anything praiseworthy—meditate on these things" (Philippians 4:8 NKJV).

Learn to look for the best in every situation. No matter what you're going through, if you look hard enough and keep the right attitude, you can find something good about the experience. If you get laid off at work, you can choose to be negative and bitter and blame God. Or, you can say, "God, I know You are in control of my life, and when one door closes, You always open a bigger and better door. So Father, I can't wait to see what You have in store for me."

When you get stuck in traffic, you can choose to be angry and impatient, or you can choose to say, "Father, You said that all things work together for good to them who love the Lord. So I thank You for guiding me and protecting me and keeping me in Your perfect will."

Keep your mind set on the good things of God.

You must make a choice to keep your mind focused on the better things. It's not going to automatically happen. You must be determined and put forth some effort if you're going to keep your mind set on the good things of God and experience His best.

We must be especially on guard during times of adversity, in times of personal challenge. When troubles strike, often the first thoughts that come to mind are not higher thoughts; they're not positive thoughts. Negative thoughts bombard us from every possible angle. Right there, we must choose to trust God and not allow ourselves to get down and discouraged or just give up.

Our mind is similar to the transmission in a car. We can choose which way we want to go by engaging the gears. It doesn't take any more effort to go forward than it does to go backward. It's all in the decision process. Similarly, we determine by our own choices which way our lives are going to go. If you choose to stay focused on the positive and keep your mind set on the good things of God, all the forces of darkness are not going to be able to keep you from moving forward and fulfilling your destiny. But if you make the mistake of dwelling on the negative, focusing on your problems and your impossibilities, it's similar to putting that car in reverse and backing away from the victory God has in store for you. You must decide which way you want to go.

Psychologists are convinced that our lives move in the direction of our most dominant thoughts. Throughout this day, engage your mind in thoughts of joy, peace, victory, abundance, and blessings, and you will move toward those things, drawing them to yourself at the same time. Now, that's a magnetic personality!

❧ Today's Prayer for Your Best Life Now ❧

Father, help me to see as much good as I can in every person and in every situation. Rather than seeing the glass half empty, let me see it as half full. I choose to have an optimistic outlook on life.

NO FEAR

Scripture Reading for Your Best Life Now   2 Corinthians 10:1–5

We are destroying speculations and every lofty thing raised up against the knowledge of God, and we are taking every thought captive to the obedience of Christ.
2 Corinthians 10:5 NASB

It is not honoring to God to go around with a nagging, negative feeling, always thinking that something is wrong. You may not even know why you do it, but you tend to think that things are never going to work out well for you. It's almost as though you have a black cloud following you around. That attitude will keep you from believing for the good things of God.

The Bible teaches us to "cast down every negative thought and every wrong imagination" (see 2 Corinthians 10:5). Yet it is so easy to slip into assuming the worst. Maybe you get a pain in your side, and the first thought that comes to your mind is, *Oh, no! That must be cancer. That's the same thing my uncle died from.* Before long, your imagination is running wild, and you are seeing yourself in all sorts of negative scenarios. If you believe it and see it in your imagination long enough, many times those negative things will come to pass.

Maybe you hear a siren some night. Your family is not at home, and the thought immediately comes to your mind, *Oh, no! Maybe*

my children have been in an accident. They're probably headed to
the hospital right now!

Right there, you must stop and make a decision. Are you going
to dwell on that lie and allow fear to have its way with you, or
will you be disciplined in your thought life and do what the Scripture says? The Bible says, "Fix your thoughts on what is true and
honorable and right. Think about things that are pure and lovely
and admirable. Think about things that are excellent and worthy
of praise" (Philippians 4:8 NLT).

Rather than thinking the worst when you hear that siren, dwell
on the fact that God has promised He will give His angels charge
over your family. Say something such as "Thank You, Father, that
Your angels are protecting my family members. Thank You that
my children are safe and sound in the palm of Your hand."

It's all too easy to give in to fear and allow your imagination to
run wild. One time early in Victoria's and my marriage, I came
home late one evening, and for some reason my garage door remote control wouldn't work. I parked outside and had walked up
to the front door when I realized I didn't have a key to that door.
I knocked and waited for Victoria to answer. No response. I
knocked again. I knew my wife was home, but she didn't answer
the door. I was puzzled.

As I listened more intently, I heard what seemed to be some unusual banging noises coming from inside our home. I got worried
and thought, *What's going on?* I knocked harder and louder, and
in return I heard still more banging.

Now my imagination began to run wild. I thought for sure that
a burglar or some intruder was in the house trying to hurt Victoria. In my mind, I could picture the struggle that was going on. A
cold sweat enveloped my body and I knew I had to do something
fast. I took off running around the house, trying to find an open
window, an open door, some way to get into our house so I could
rescue Victoria. I couldn't find any way in. By now, I was nearly
in a panic. I was desperate. I ran out back, where I found a large

log, which I quickly grabbed and lugged around to the front door. I planned to use the log as a battering ram to break down our front door. (I'd seen people do this in Western movies!)

Just as I got to the door and was about to plow through it, Victoria opened the door. She was smiling and happy-go-lucky. Then she saw me, standing there all sweaty, lugging a filthy dirty log. She said, "Joel, what in the world are you doing with that log?"

God honors faith.

"Well, I heard all the banging. I thought something was wrong. I was coming to rescue you."

"I don't know what you're going to rescue me from," Victoria said with a laugh. "I was just upstairs hanging some pictures on the wall."

I could have saved myself a lot of trouble (and probably saved a few years off my life, too) if I had cast down those wrong imaginations. I'd have been much better off if I had not given in to fear and worry.

Always remember: God honors faith; the enemy attacks with fear. Maybe your business has been a little slow, and in your imagination you've already seen it going under. You've seen the creditors coming and shutting it down. No, instead, cast down those wrong imaginations and start seeing your business turn around.

Perhaps you've been struggling in your marriage, and in your mind you've already seen yourself divorced and living single. No, take those thoughts captive, and change what you're seeing.

Maybe you received a bad report from the doctor, and you've already seen your health failing. You've practically planned your own funeral. No, quit allowing all those negative imaginations to play destructive games with you. This is war! You must take those thoughts captive, and then cast them out of your thinking patterns.

What's showing on the screen of your mind? Do you see yourself as strong, happy, healthy, rising to new heights? Or do you see yourself as defeated, failing, always struggling? Get your mind going in the right direction. Develop the habit of staying positive in your thoughts and conversations. Live in faith, not in fear. Make a decision today that you will no longer give in to negative worries and fears, but instead you will think on things that are pure and wholesome and of good report. If you will do your part, God will keep you in perfect peace.

✆ Today's Prayer for Your Best Life Now ✆

Please forgive me, Father, for allowing fear and worry to dominate my thoughts. I am Your child, and I know that Your power working in me is greater than what anyone or anything can do against me. I will trust in You today.

CHANGING THE FLOW

There is a river whose streams make glad the city of God, the holy dwelling places of the Most High.

PSALM 46:4 NASB

WHEN YOUR THOUGHTS have been running in a certain pattern for a long period of time, it's as though they have been eroding a deep riverbed, and the water can flow in only one direction. Imagine a person who habitually leans toward negative thinking month after month, year after year. With every pessimistic thought, they dig that riverbed a bit deeper. The flow accelerates, growing stronger as it goes. After a period of time, the water is flowing so strongly, every thought that comes out of the river is negative. That person has programmed his or her mind into a negative thinking pattern.

Fortunately, we can cause a new river to flow, one going in a positive direction. When you dwell on God's Word and start seeing the best in situations, little by little, one thought at a time, you are redirecting the flow of that river. At first, just a little water will trickle out of the negative stream into the positive stream. It may not look like much at first, but as you continue to reject negative thoughts and redirect the flow, as you choose faith instead of fear, expecting good things and taking control of your thought life, that negative stream will dwindle and the positive river will flow with much greater force. If you'll keep it up, that old stream will dry up, and you will discover a whole new river flowing with positive, faith-filled thoughts of victory.

Occasionally, you may be tempted to mull over discouraging thoughts. In the old days, you'd go back to the same old negative river and say, "Oh, my. What in the world am I going to do? God, how am I going to get out of this mess?"

But not this time; you have a new river flowing. You can rise up and say, "No, greater is He that is in me than he that is in the world. I can do all things through Christ, and I'm coming out of this."

Start tapping into the new river, and every time you do, you will establish that new, positive river a little deeper, and the fresh water will flow more freely.

Negative thoughts assail you: *You're never going to get out of debt. You're never going to be successful. You're always going to live in poverty and lack.*

In the old days, you'd go back to that depressing river and say, "Well, yes, my family has always been poor. Nobody has ever amounted to anything. I guess it's just my lot in life."

But not this time. Now, you can go back to that positive river of faith. You can say, "I thank You, Father, that You called me to be the head, not the tail. I'm above and not beneath. You said that I will be able to lend money and not have to borrow. You said that whatever I put my hands to do shall prosper. So Father, I thank You that I am blessed, and I cannot be cursed."

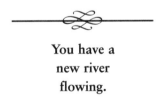

You have a new river flowing.

Friend, don't be passive, sitting back and allowing negative, critical, pessimistic thoughts to influence your life. The Bible tells us that we need to be "transformed by the renewing of our minds" (see Romans 12:1–2). If you will transform your thinking, God will transform your life.

Keep in mind, though, that river of negativity wasn't formed overnight, nor will it be redirected without some conscious, strenuous effort on your part. God will help you, but you are going to have to make quality decisions every day, choosing the good, rejecting the bad. Determine to keep your mind set on the good things of God. Right now you can say, "Father, I'm excited about today. This is a day You have made; I'm going to rejoice and be glad in it. God, I know You reward those who seek You, so I thank You in advance for Your blessings, favor, and victory in my life today." Then go out and live your best life now.

❧ Today's Prayer for Your Best Life Now ❧

Starting today, Father, I am going to begin changing the flow of my thoughts. From now on, I will choose to align my thinking with Your Word. When I tend to be negative, please show me the error of my way, so I can redirect the flow in the proper direction.

A CAN-DO MENTALITY

SCRIPTURE READING FOR YOUR BEST LIFE NOW   Isaiah 55:6–11

*I can do everything with the help of Christ who gives
me the strength I need.*

PHILIPPIANS 4:13 NLT

WE DRAW TO our lives that which we constantly think about. If
we dwell on the negative, we will attract negative people, experiences, and attitudes. If we dwell on our fears, we will draw in
more fear. You set the direction of your life with your thoughts.

The choice is up to you. You don't have to entertain every
thought that comes to mind. The first thing you need to do is as-
certain where that thought is coming from. Is that thought from
God, is it your own thought, or is it a destructive thought from the
enemy?

If a thought is negative, most likely it's from the enemy. If it's a
discouraging, destructive thought; if it brings fear, worry, doubt,
or unbelief; if the thought makes you feel weak, inadequate, or insecure, I can guarantee you that thought is not from God. You
need to deal with it immediately.

The Bible says, "We should cast down every wrong imagination
and take into captivity every wrong thought" (see 2 Corinthians
10:5). That simply means: Don't dwell on it. Get rid of it immediately. Reject it, and choose to think on something positive. If
you make the mistake of dwelling on the enemy's lies, you allow

the negative seed to take root. And the more you think about it, the more it's going to grow, creating an enemy stronghold in your mind from which attacks can be launched. Night and day, the enemy will pummel your mind with notions such as: *You're never going to be successful. Nobody in your family has ever amounted to much. You're not smart enough. Your parents were poor. Your grandmother was always depressed. Your grandfather couldn't keep a job. Even your pet dog was always sick! You were just born into the wrong family.*

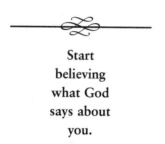

Start believing what God says about you.

If you believe those kinds of lies, you will set limits in your life that will be nearly impossible to rise above. You must get in the habit of casting down the thoughts of the enemy and start believing what God says about you. God is not limited by your family tree. He is not limited by your education, your social standing, your economic status, or your race. No, the only thing that limits God is your lack of faith.

There is no such thing as the wrong side of the tracks with our God. If you will put your trust in Him, God will make your life significant. God longs to make something great out of your life. He'll take a nobody and shape that person into a somebody. But you must cooperate with God's plan; you must start thinking of yourself as the champion God made you to be.

The enemy attacks your mind saying that you don't have what it takes; God says you do have what it takes. Whom are you going to believe? The enemy says you're not able to succeed; God says you can do all things through Christ. The enemy says you'll never get out of debt; God says not only are you going to get out of debt, you will lend and not borrow. The enemy says you're never going to get well; God says He will restore your health. The enemy says you'll never amount to anything; God says He will raise you up and make your life significant. The enemy says your problems are too big, there's no hope; God says He will solve those problems. Not only that, but He will turn those problems around and use them for your good.

Friend, develop a habit of believing what God says about you; start agreeing with godly thoughts. God's thoughts will fill you with faith, hope, and victory. God's thoughts will build you up and encourage you. They will give you the strength you need to keep on keeping on. God's thoughts will give you that can-do mentality.

How can you discover God's thoughts? Easy, just start reading and meditating on His Word, allowing its truths to become the operating system for your life.

Today's Prayer for Your Best Life Now

Father, I choose to think in patterns that will be pleasing to You. Help me, I pray, to recognize those areas where the enemy is trying to make inroads into my mind. Please help me to cast down every evil thought and imagination, and to replace those negative ideas with input from Your Word.

REPROGRAM YOUR COMPUTER

SCRIPTURE READING FOR YOUR BEST LIFE NOW   Deuteronomy 30:11–20

Incline your ear and hear the words of the wise, and apply your mind to my knowledge; for it will be pleasant if you keep them within you, that they may be ready on your lips. So that your trust may be in the LORD.

PROVERBS 22:17–19 NASB

You've HEARD IT many times before: Your mind is similar to a computer. But what we often fail to consider is the fact that what you program into your computer will dictate how well it will function. How foolish it would be to complain, "I hate this computer! It never gives me the right answer; it never does what I want it to do." Think about it: You can have the most powerful computer in the world, but if you program it with the wrong software or with misinformation, it will not be able to function as the manufacturer intended.

Beyond that, there is now a myriad of computer viruses lurking in cyberspace, waiting for an opportunity to destroy your hard drive and the information stored in your computer. Such viruses can get into a perfectly good computer and contaminate the software. Before long the computer will develop a sluggishness; it will malfunction. You may not be able to get to the programs you need or retrieve important documents. All too often, you unwittingly pass along the virus to a friend, family member, or business associate, exacerbating the problem by contaminating their systems with the same virus that infected yours. Usually these problems occur not because the computer is defective, but because somebody has reprogrammed the software or contaminated good, valuable programs or information within.

Similarly, too often we allow negative thoughts, words, and other devious viruses to access our minds, subtly changing our software or corrupting our operating system, information, and values. We were created in the image of God. Before we were ever formed, He programmed us to live abundant lives, to be happy, healthy, and whole. But when our thinking becomes contaminated, it is no longer in line with God's Word. We make serious mistakes and wrong choices. We go through life with low self-esteem, worries, fears, feelings of inadequacy and insecurity. Making matters worse, we pass on our negative attitudes to others.

When you recognize these things happening, you must reprogram your computer. You must change your thinking. Understand, *you* are not defective. God made you, and He has programmed you for victory. But until you get your thinking in line with your owner's manual, God's Word, you will never operate to your full potential.

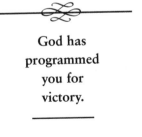

God has programmed you for victory.

The Bible says, "I have set before you life and death, blessings and curses, positive and negative; therefore, God says choose life" (see Deuteronomy 30:19). This is not a once-and-for-all matter. It's a choice we have to make on a moment-by-moment basis. We must choose to dwell on the positive, choose to think on the good. The negative is always going to be around us. We have to choose to dwell on what's right, rather than on what's wrong. Choose to focus on what you have, not on what you don't have. Choose to think the right thoughts.

You cannot prevent negative thoughts from knocking at your door, but you can control whether or not you copy those thoughts onto your mental "hard drive." If you will stand guard over that entrance and keep your mind focused on the good things of God, the Bible says that "God will keep you in perfect peace" (see Isaiah 26:3). You can have peace in the midst of your storms if you'll simply learn to choose the right thoughts. Dwell on the fact that Almighty God is on your side. Stand on the fact that He's promised to fight your battles for you. Dwell on the truth that no weapon formed against you can prosper. If you start thinking these kinds of thoughts, you will be filled with faith and confidence, no matter what comes against you today.

❧ Today's Prayer for Your Best Life Now ❧

Father, I get shaken up so easily by events in the world and in my life. Please help me to keep my mind centered on You, and on the truth of Your Word. Help me to have a positive, faith-filled attitude in the midst of difficult days as well as the good days.

ON THE EDGE OF YOUR PROMISED LAND

Scripture Reading for Your Best Life Now   Genesis 37:1–11

Thou wilt keep him in perfect peace, whose mind is stayed on thee: because he trusteth in thee.

ISAIAH 26:3 KJV

ONE OF THE most important bits of information that you need to reinstall in your mental computer is that you are a victor and not a victim. The Scripture teaches, "If God is for you, who can be against you?" (see Romans 8:31).

When negative, discouraging thoughts come, cast them down immediately, and make a conscious choice to dwell on what God says about you. For instance, a thought comes to you that you're getting sick or that you have some serious disease. Refuse to dwell on that thought. Just say, "Father, I thank You that You are restoring health unto me. I thank You that I'm going to live and not die, that I will declare the works of the Lord."

Or perhaps a thought comes to you that you are not going to get that promotion you have been seeking, or you're not going to get that big contract. Reject that sort of thinking and declare instead, "Father, You said that no good thing will You withhold when I walk uprightly. You said when I am obedient Your blessings will chase me down and overtake me, so I thank You that You've got good things in store."

Reprogram one thought at a time by going back to the original manual (the Bible), where you will discover that God always causes you to triumph. God said whatever you put your hands to is going to prosper and succeed. He says that you are blessed and cannot be cursed. People may try to tell you that your dreams aren't going to come to pass, that you are not able to go any further in life. But don't believe those lies. God said you are well able to fulfill your destiny.

When you go through disappointments in life—and we all do—or when you face a setback and it looks as though one of your dreams has died, keep believing. When it looks dark and dreary and you don't see any way out, remind yourself that your heavenly Father created the whole universe. He is in control of your life, guiding and directing your steps. His plans for you are good and not evil. Don't make the mistake of sitting around feeling sorry for yourself. No, put on a fresh new attitude. Take what God has given you and make the most of it. You know the truth; it's time to allow that truth to set you free.

Recall the Old Testament account of how the children of Israel were camped right next door to the Promised Land. They were so excited, they couldn't wait to enter the land flowing with milk and honey. All they had to do was go in and fight for the land. Beyond that, God had promised them the victory, and He had proved His ability to come through for His people.

God had parted the Red Sea and brought them through on dry land. He had supernaturally fed them manna in the barren wilderness. You'd think they would have been filled with faith, primed and ready to drive their enemies out of the Promised Land. But no, they said, "It's impossible. It's never going to happen." Their negative thinking kept them from ever going into the Promised Land.

Maybe you are camped right next door to your Promised Land. God has great things He wants to do in your life. He wants to promote you. He wants to increase you. He may want to heal your body, to restore your marriage, or to bless you financially. Maybe you are right on the edge of a miracle! Don't allow a lack of faith or a wrong mind-set to rob you of your destiny.

If you will get your thinking lined up with God's thinking, nothing will be able to stop you. No obstacle will be too high, no situation too difficult. If you believe God's Word, all things are possible.

Remember, the enemy always fights the hardest when he knows God has something great in store for you. The darkest battle, the darkest storm will always give way to the brightest sunrise. Keep believing, keep praying, keep pressing forward. The Scripture says, "Don't get tired of doing what's right, for in due season you shall reap if you faint not" (see Galatians 6:9). It may

The enemy always fights the hardest when he knows God has something great in store for you.

be hard right now, but remind yourself that you have the power of God inside you. You can do what you need to do.

I remember when my father went to be with the Lord back in 1999. I knew deep inside that I was to pastor Lakewood Church, but I had preached only one time prior to Daddy's death. I was camped next door to my Promised Land, but all I could see were the giants, the reasons why I couldn't do it. I thought, *God, I don't feel qualified. I don't feel like I have enough experience; I've never been to seminary.* All sorts of negative thoughts bombarded my mind. The critics talked about how Lakewood was never going to make it, that the church was sure to go under. I heard all these negative reports, and I had to make the decision of whether I was going to agree with men or go with God. Was I going to shrink back into my comfort zone where it was safe, or was I going to step out in faith, knowing that Almighty God was on my side? I decided to go with God.

But it wasn't easy. As soon as I'd get up in the morning, negative thoughts would pummel my mind. *Joel, you made a huge mistake. You're going to get up there and make a fool out of yourself. You don't even know how to preach.*

I'd say, "No, I'm not going to dwell on that. I know I am well able to do what God has called me to do." Still, when I first started speaking in public I needed to hold on to the podium; I was so nervous. Several Sunday mornings I got up and thought, *I can't do this!* But I'd go stand before the mirror, look myself right in the eyes, and say, "Joel, you are strong in the Lord and in the power of His might. You are anointed. Greater is He that is in you than he that is in the world."

What was I doing? I was reprogramming my computer. The Bible says, "Let the weak say I'm strong. Let the sick say I am well." Maybe you, too, need to go stand before that mirror and start talking to yourself. Start speaking words of faith and victory into your life. The Scripture says, "This book of the law should not depart out of your mouth but you should meditate on it day and night. Then you will prosper and have good success" (see Joshua 1:8).

✖ Today's Prayer for Your Best Life Now ✖

Father, I am going to dare to believe what You say about me, rather than what anyone else says. Please help me to fill my mind with thoughts that are pleasing to You, thoughts that will cause me to progress all the way to my Promised Land.

LET GOD FIGHT YOUR BATTLES

Scripture Reading for Your Best Life Now   2 Chronicles 32:1–8

When a man's ways are pleasing to the LORD, He makes
even his enemies to be at peace with him.

PROVERBS 16:7 NASB

IF YOU WILL trust in God, He'll fight your battles for you. It
doesn't matter what you're going through, or how big your oppo-
nents are. Keep an attitude of faith. Stay calm. Stay at peace. Stay
in a positive frame of mind. And don't try to do it all your own
way. Let God do it His way. If you will simply obey His commands, He will change things in your favor.

You may be going through great difficulties, and you're
tempted to think, *I'm never going to get out of this. This is never
going to change. I'm never going to win in this situation.*

No, the Bible says, "Don't get weary and faint in your mind"
(see Hebrews 12:3). Remember, you must first win the battle in
your mind. Stand strong. When negative thoughts come, reject
them and replace them with God's thoughts. When you're in that
attitude of faith, you are opening the door for God to work in
your situation. You may not see anything happening with your
natural eyes, but don't let that discourage you. In the unseen
realm, in the spiritual world, God is at work. He is changing
things in your favor. And if you'll do your part and keep believ-

ing, in due season, at the right time, God will bring you out with the victory.

The key is to choose the right thoughts, to keep your mind set. Not just when you feel good, not just when things are going your

In due season, at the right time, God will bring you out with the victory.

way, not just when you don't have any problems, but even in the tough times of life—especially in the difficult times—you must keep your mind set on the good things of God. Stay full of faith. Stay full of joy. Stay full of hope. Make a conscious decision that you are going to stay in a positive frame of mind.

Some people take one step forward and then two steps backward. They are happy and in a good attitude one day, then the next day they are negative and depressed. They make a little progress, then they back up. Because of their vacillating faith, they never really get to the place God wants them to be. They never experience the victories He has in store for them.

Friend, you must be consistent. Your attitude should be: *I refuse to go backward. I am going forward with God. I'm going to be the person He wants me to be. I'm going to fulfill my destiny.*

If you will maintain that mind-set, God will continually work in your life. He'll fight your battles for you. He'll give you peace in the midst of a storm, and He'll help you live that life of victory He has in store for you.

✎ Today's Prayer for Your Best Life Now ✎

Thank You, Father, that I am not alone in this life. You are with me, no matter what challenge I am facing, and You help me to take that next step of obedience. Today, I will trust You to fight my battles as I move forward in my life.

SPEAK TO YOUR MOUNTAINS

Truly I say to you, whoever says to this mountain, "Be taken up and cast into the sea," and does not doubt in his heart, but believes that what he says is going to happen, it shall be granted him. Therefore I say to you, all things for which you pray and ask, believe that you have received them, and they shall be granted you.

MARK 11:23–24 NASB

IF YOU'RE IN a tough situation today, now more than ever you need to guard what you say and not allow any negative, destructive words to come out of your mouth. Scripture says, "Death and life are in the power of the tongue; and you will eat the fruit thereof" (see Proverbs 18:21). In other words, you create an environment for either good or evil with your words, and you are going to have to live in that world you've created. If you're always murmuring, complaining, and talking about how bad life is treating you, you're going to live in a pretty miserable, depressing world. You will always be tempted to use your words to describe negative situations, but God wants us to use our words to *change* our negative situations. Don't talk about the problem, talk about the solution.

The Bible instructs us to speak to our mountains (see Mark 11:23–24). Maybe your mountain is a sickness; perhaps it is a troubled relationship; maybe your mountain is a floundering business. Whatever your mountain is, you must do more than think about it, more than pray about it; you must speak to that obstacle. The Bible says, "Let the weak say I'm strong. Let the oppressed say I'm free. Let the sick say I'm healed. Let the poor say I'm well off" (see Joel 3:10).

Start talking to your mountains about how big your God is!

Start calling yourself healed, happy, whole, blessed, and prosperous. Stop talking to God about how big your mountains are, and start talking to your mountains about how big your God is!

When David faced the giant Goliath, he didn't murmur and complain and say, "God, why do I always have these huge problems?" He didn't dwell on the fact that Goliath was three times his size. Nor did he dwell on the fact that Goliath was a skilled warrior and he was just a shepherd boy. He didn't focus on the magnitude of the obstacle before him. He chose instead to focus on the greatness of his God. He changed his whole atmosphere through the words that came out of his mouth.

David looked Goliath right in the eyes, and with great determination, he said, "Listen, Goliath, you come against me with a sword and a shield, but I come against you in the name of the Lord God of Israel" (see 1 Samuel 17:45).

Now, those are words of faith! Notice, too, that he spoke the words aloud. He didn't merely *think* them; he didn't simply *pray* them. He spoke directly to the mountain of a man in front of him, and said, "I will defeat you and feed your flesh to the birds of the air this very day." And with God's help, he did exactly that!

When you are facing obstacles in your path, you must boldly say, "Greater is He who is in me than he who is in the world [see 1 John 4:4]. No weapon formed against me is going to prosper [see Isaiah 54:17]. God always causes me to triumph." Quit complaining about poverty and lack and start declaring, "God supplies all of my needs in abundance." Quit nagging that friend or family member who is not serving God and start declaring, "As for me and my house, we will serve the LORD" (Joshua 24:15 NASB). Quit complaining that nothing good ever happens to you and start declaring, "Everything I touch prospers and succeeds." We must stop cursing the darkness. Let's start commanding the light to come.

Friend, there is a miracle in your mouth. If you want to change your world, start today by changing your words.

✆ Today's Prayer for Your Best Life Now ✆

Father, I want to speak words that are consistent with Your Word; may my words be filled continually with faith and hope, and may they create an environment in which You can do great and mighty things in and through my life!

HEALING WORDS

My son, give attention to my words; incline your ear to my sayings. Do not let them depart from your eyes; keep them in the midst of your heart; for they are life to those who find them, and health to all their flesh.

PROVERBS 4:20–22 NKJV

SOME STORIES BEAR repeating over and over because they build our faith. For instance, God's people often retold the Exodus story, partly because God instructed them to do so, but in my mind, I can also imagine them telling the story of Moses and the deliverance from Egyptian slavery for the sheer joy they experienced in passing on the events to the next generation. In some ways, I feel the same way when I tell about my mother's miraculous healing.

In 1981, my mother was diagnosed with cancer and given just a few weeks to live. I'll never forget what a shock that news was to our family. Mother was hospitalized for twenty-one days, while the doctors ran test after test. Finally, they called my dad out into the hallway and said, "Pastor, we hate to tell you this, but your wife has only a few weeks to live. Not months, weeks . . ." So they basically sent our mom home to die.

But my mother never gave up. She refused to speak words of defeat. She didn't complain about how sick or weak she felt, or how awful her life was, or how hopeless her situation looked. No, she chose to put God's words in her mind and in her mouth.

She started speaking positively about her health and calling in her healing. All during the day, we'd hear Mother going through the house speaking aloud, "I will live and not die, and I will declare the works of the Lord" (see Psalm 118:17).

I'd say, "Mother, how are you doing?"

She'd say, "Joel, I'm strong in the Lord and the power of His might." She pored over her Bible and found about thirty or forty favorite passages of Scripture concerning healing. She wrote them down, and every day, she'd read over them and boldly declare, "With long life, He satisfies me and shows me His salvation."

As Mother mixed her words with God's Words, something powerful began to happen. Her circumstances began to change. Not overnight, but little by little, she began to feel better. She got her appetite back and started gaining weight. Slowly but surely, her strength returned. A few weeks went by and Mother got a little better. A few months went by, and she was even better. A few years went by, and she just kept on confessing God's Word. Today, it has been more than twenty years since we received the report that Mother had just a few weeks to live, and Mother remains cancer-free, healed by the power of God and His Word! And she is still confessing God's Word. She gets up every morning, reviews those same Scriptures, and still speaks those words of faith, victory, and health over her life.

> God is a miracle-working God.

My mother used her words to change her world, and you can do the same thing. Maybe you are facing a "hopeless" situation. Don't give up. God is a miracle-working God. He knows what you're going through, and He will not let you down. Start speaking words of faith today, and watch how God causes your circumstances to change.

≫ Today's Prayer for Your Best Life Now ≫

Father, it is Your Word that I rely upon to bring healing and health to my life and to those for whom I am praying. I'm not interested in spiritual tricks or formulas; I only want Your will to be done. May my words reflect Your words and Your will in the situations I am facing. I will dare to speak faith-filled words today.

SPEAKING WORDS OF FAITH

SCRIPTURE READING FOR YOUR BEST LIFE NOW   Deuteronomy 7:6–15

Be strong in the Lord and in his mighty power.
EPHESIANS 6:10 NIV

Oᴜʀ ᴡᴏʀᴅs ᴀʀᴇ vital in bringing our dreams to pass. It's not enough to see your dreams simply by faith or in your imagination. You have to begin speaking words of faith over your life. The moment you speak something out, you give birth to it. This is a spiritual principle, and it works whether what you are saying is good or bad, positive or negative.

In that regard, many times we are our own worst enemies. We blame everybody and everything else, but the truth is, we are profoundly influenced by what we say about ourselves. Scripture says, "We are snared by the words of our mouths" (see Proverbs 6:2).

"Nothing good ever happens to me." "My life is a disaster." "My dreams never come to pass." "I knew I wouldn't get promoted." Statements such as these will literally prevent you from moving ahead in life. That's why you must learn to guard your tongue and speak only faith-filled words over your life. Simply put, your words can either make you or break you.

God never commanded us to repeatedly verbalize our pain and suffering. He didn't instruct us to go around discussing our negative situations, airing our "dirty laundry" with all our friends and neighbors. Instead, God told us to speak constantly of His good-ness, to speak of His promises in the morning at the breakfast table, in the evenings around the dinner table, at night before bed-time, continually dwelling on the good things of God.

Use your words to *change* your situation.

You could experience a new sense of joy in your home, if you'd simply stop talking about the negative things in your life and begin talking about God's Word.

If you are always talking about your problems, don't be surprised if you live in perpetual defeat. If you're in the habit of saying, "Nothing good ever happens to me," guess what? Nothing good is going to happen to you! You must stop talking about the problem and start talking about the solution. Quit speaking words of defeat, and start speaking words of victory. Don't use your words to describe your situation; use your words to *change* your situation.

Set the tone for the entire day as soon as you get out of bed. If you wait until you have read the morning newspaper, you'll start your day with all sorts of sad, dreary news. Try starting your day with some good news by speaking God's Word over your life! The moment you wake up, begin to give new life to your dreams by speaking words of faith and victory.

Understand, avoiding negative talk is not enough. That's simi-lar to a football team having a good defense but no offense. If your team is constantly playing defense, you stand little chance of scoring. You must get the ball and move it down the field; you must get on the offense. You have to be aggressive.

Similarly, you must start using your words to move forward in life, to bring to life the great things God has in store for you. The Scripture says, "With the heart one believes unto righteousness, and with the mouth confession is made unto salvation" (Romans 10:10 NKJV). This same principle is true in other areas. When you believe God's Word and begin to speak it, mixing it with your faith, you are actually confirming that truth and making it valid in your own life.

If you are facing sickness today, you should confirm God's Word concerning healing. Say something such as, "Father, I thank You that You are my healer, and that You promised me in Psalm 118 that I will live and not die and I will declare the works of the Lord." As you boldly declare it, you are confirming that truth in your own life.

Friend, when you make those kinds of bold declarations, all heaven comes to attention to back up God's Word.

❧ Today's Prayer for Your Best Life Now ❧

Thank You, Father that I can align my words with Your Word. Today I am speaking words of victory, health, and success about my life, that I will be strong spiritually, that my body will be well, and that my life will have eternal significance.

THE VALUE OF BLESSING

The word is very near you, in your mouth and in your heart, that you may observe it.

DEUTERONOMY 30:14 NASB

NEGATIVE WORDS CAN destroy a person. You cannot speak negatively about someone on one hand, then turn around and expect that person to be blessed. If you want your son or daughter to be productive and successful, you need to begin declaring words of life over your children rather than predictions of doom and despair. The Scripture reminds us that with our words we can bless people or we can curse them (see James 3:10).

In the Old Testament, the people clearly understood the power of the blessing. As the family patriarch approached senility or death, the oldest sons gathered alongside their father. The father would then lay his hands on each son's head and speak loving, faith-filled words over them about their future. These pronouncements comprised what was known ever after as "the blessing." The family realized that these were more than Dad's dying wishes; these words carried spiritual authority and had the ability to bring success, prosperity, and health into their future.

Many times, children even fought over the father's blessing. They weren't fighting over money that they might inherit. Nor were they arguing over the family business. No, they were fighting over faith-filled words. They realized that if they received the father's blessing, wealth and success would be a natural by-product. Beyond that, they deeply desired the blessing from someone they loved and respected.

One of the most amazing biblical records concerning the power of the blessing comes out of the lives of Jacob and Esau, the two sons of Isaac (see Genesis 27:1–41). Jacob wanted his father's blessing—not just any blessing, but the blessing that rightfully belonged to the firstborn son in the family. Isaac was old, near death, and he was practically blind. One day he called to his son Esau and said, "Go kill some game, and prepare me a meal and I will give you the blessing that belongs to the firstborn son." But Jacob's mother, Rebekah, overheard this conversation. Rebekah loved Jacob more than she loved Esau, so she told Jacob to put on Esau's clothes in an attempt to trick Isaac into giving him the blessing. Then she prepared one of Isaac's favorite meals.

While Esau was out in the field hunting, she said to Jacob, "Go to your father and present him this food. And he'll give you the blessing that really belongs to your brother."

Jacob understood that he was risking his entire future on this gambit. He recognized that the words his father spoke over him would impact him, for either good or evil, the rest of his life.

Speak words that encourage, inspire, and motivate.

Whether we realize it or not, our words affect our children's future for either good or evil. Our words have the same kind of power that Isaac's words had. We need to speak loving words of approval and acceptance, words that encourage, inspire, and motivate our family members to reach for new heights. When we do that, we are speaking blessings into their lives, and they will indeed be blessed.

⟨⟩ Today's Prayer for Your Best Life Now ⟨⟩

Help me to understand, Father, the tremendous value in blessing others—my family members, coworkers, and others with whom I have an influence. Then help me to speak words of blessing concerning their lives, words that open doors of opportunity rather than shutting them.

BLESS THE CHILDREN

Scripture Reading for Your Best Life Now   Isaiah 49:14–23

The LORD gave me a message. He said, "I knew you before I formed you in your mother's womb. Before you were born I set you apart and appointed you as my spokesman to the world."

JEREMIAH 1:4–5 NLT

MOST PARENTS WANT the best for their children, yet too often, we slip into being harsh and critical with our children, constantly finding fault in something our children are doing. "Why can't you make better grades?" "You didn't mow the lawn right." "Go clean your room—it looks like a pigpen!" "You can't do anything right, can you?"

Such negative words will cause our children to lose the sense of value God has placed within them. As parents, we have a responsibility before God and society to train our children, to discipline them when they disobey, to lovingly correct them when they make wrong choices. But we should not constantly harp on our kids. If you continually speak words that discourage and dishearten, before long you will destroy your child's self-image. And with your negative words, you will open a door, allowing the enemy to bring all kinds of insecurity and inferiority into your child's life. Millions of adults today are still suffering as a result of the negative words their parents spoke over them as children.

If you speak negative words over your children, you are cursing their future. Moreover, God will hold you responsible for destroying their destiny. With authority comes responsibility, and you have the responsibility as the spiritual authority over your child to make sure that he feels loved, accepted, and approved.

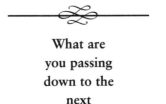

What are you passing down to the next generation?

Beyond that, most children get their concepts of who God is and what He is like from their fathers. If the father is mean, critical, and harsh, inevitably the children will grow up with a distorted view of God. If the father is loving, kind, compassionate, and just, the children will better understand God's character.

One of the reasons I talk so much about the goodness of God is because I saw it modeled by my dad. Nobody could have represented God any better to us Osteen kids than my dad did. Even when we made mistakes or got off track, while Daddy was firm, he was also loving and kind. He nurtured us back to the right course. He never beat us into line; he loved us onto the right path. Although he was very busy, he always took time for us. He encouraged us to do great things, to fulfill our dreams.

My siblings and I were not perfect kids. We made plenty of mistakes. But my parents never focused on our weaknesses or on the problems. They always focused on the solutions. They constantly told us we were the best kids in the world. And we grew up secure, knowing that our parents not only loved each other, but they loved us and believed in us. They were going to stand behind us through thick and thin. We knew they were never going to criticize or condemn us, but would always believe the best in us.

Now, as a father myself, I'm practicing the same sort of things with my children. I'm speaking words of blessing into their lives that will be passed down to another generation. And I know my children will pass down the goodness of God to their children, and on and on.

Before they go to bed, Victoria and I tell our children, "There's nothing you can't do. You have a bright future in front of you. You're surrounded by God's favor. Everything you touch is going to prosper."

Victoria and I believe that we have an opportunity and a responsibility to speak God's blessings into our children now, while they are young. Why should we wait till they are teenagers, or in their twenties and about to get married, to begin praying for God's blessings in their lives? No, we're declaring God's blessings over them all the days of their lives. And we are convinced that our words will impact our children long after they are grown and have children of their own.

What are you passing down to the next generation? It's not enough to think it; you must vocalize it. A blessing is not a blessing until it is spoken. Your children need to hear you say words such as, "I love you. I believe in you. I think you're great. There's nobody else like you. You are one of a kind." They need to hear your approval. They need to feel your love. They need your blessing. Start speaking those blessings over your family members today.

✺ Today's Prayer for Your Best Life Now ✺

Heavenly Father, please help me to speak words of blessing into the lives of my children, as well as other children You allow to grace my life. Today, I choose to see the good, the positive things in those around me, rather than the negative, and I will reinforce and encourage those things that honor You.

PART FOUR

LET GO OF THE PAST

SHAKE IT OFF

Through the LORD's mercies we are not consumed, because His compassions fail not. They are new every morning; great is Your faithfulness.

LAMENTATIONS 3:22–23 NKJV

EVERYBODY GOES THROUGH disappointments and setbacks from time to time, but if we hold on to hurt and pain, we end up living negative and bitter lives. Maybe you've made some mistakes or some poor choices, and now you're tempted to sit around feeling guilty and condemned thinking something such as:

- "I wish I had been a better parent."
- "I wish I had gone back to school."
- "I wish I had chosen another career."
- "I wish I had married that other person."

It's so easy to live life focused on that rearview mirror. We can't do anything about the past, and we have no guarantees regarding the future; we can only do something about right now.

The good news is, your past does not have to poison your future.

Maybe you've made some mistakes, or you've had some unfair things happen to you. Maybe one of your dreams didn't work out. God still has good things in store for you. He wants to take that negative situation, turn it around, and use it to your advantage.

Today can be a new beginning.

When you get up each morning, one of the first things you should do is shake off the disappointments of yesterday. Discard discouragement, guilt, and condemnation. Your attitude should be, *It's a new day, and I'm not going to drag the hurts of yesterday into this day. I'm going to start afresh.*

The Scripture says that God's mercies are new every morning. You may have made a lot of mistakes, but God has not run out of mercy. He makes a fresh new batch every single morning. Do you know why? Because He knew we were going to use up all that He made yesterday!

You may have done something last week that you're not proud of, but you don't have to carry that around with you any longer. You simply need to receive God's mercy and forgiveness. Today can be a new beginning.

Friend, don't be a prisoner of the past. Some people are always dwelling on their disappointments. They just can't understand why their prayers aren't being answered, why their loved one wasn't healed, why they were mistreated. They don't realize it, but they're allowing their past to poison their future. God has a new beginning in store for them. He wants to restore what's been stolen, but they won't let go of the past.

If you're not willing to let go of the old, don't expect God to do the new. If you've had some unfair things happen to you, make a decision that you're going to quit reliving those things in your memory. Instead, think on good things, things that will build you up and not tear you down, things that will encourage you and give you the hope that there's a brighter tomorrow.

Why? Because your life is going to follow your thoughts. If you're constantly dwelling on all the negative things that have happened to you, focused on the mistakes you've made and what you've done wrong, then you're perpetuating that problem. Let it go. Seek forgiveness from anyone you have hurt. Forgive the people who have hurt you, release any bitterness you have been harboring, and forgive yourself. If you're going to go forward in life, you must quit looking backward.

❧ Today's Prayer for Your Best Life Now ❧

I thank You, Father, that my future happiness and fulfillment are not determined by the pains of the past. Thank You that Your mercies are new every morning. Today, I choose to believe that You have good things in store for me.

DON'T GO THERE

SCRIPTURE READING FOR YOUR BEST LIFE NOW   2 Corinthians 5:6–21

You will know the truth, and the truth will make you free.

JOHN 8:32 NASB

WHEN WE KEEP reliving the painful memories of the past, we negate God's desire to bring healing. Just as we are about to heal, we start talking about our painful experience again. We bring it up to our friends. We start reliving it, seeing it in our imagination. All of a sudden, we can feel those same emotions all over again, as though we were tearing open the old wound. It will never properly heal until we learn to leave it alone. When you dwell on painful experiences in your past, your emotions go right back there with you, and you feel the pain in the present. You can relive something in your mind and feel it today just as vividly as when it happened twenty years ago.

In my book *Your Best Life Now*, I told the full story of an experience I had a few years after my father passed away in 1999. I was over at my parents' home, and I was all alone in the house. I hadn't been there by myself in quite some time, and as I was walking through the den, for no apparent reason I started thinking about the night that my dad died. Daddy had a heart attack right there in that same room. In my imagination, I could see it all happening. I could see Daddy on the floor. I could see the paramedics working on him. I could see the look on my dad's face, and I began to feel those same emotions of despair, sadness, and discouragement that I had known the night Daddy died.

Finally, I caught myself and thought, *What am I doing? Where is my mind going? Where are these emotions taking me?*

I had to make a decision that I was not going to allow myself to relive that night. Rather than dwelling on the hurt from the past, I purposely started recalling all the good times that my dad and I had known in that den. I smiled as I remembered how we used to watch the TV show *Wheel of Fortune* together in that room. In my mind, I could see Daddy playing with our children in that den. I recalled how sometimes I'd walk into the den and Daddy would be in his favorite chair. He'd look up and say, "Joel, tell me all you know. It'll just take a second." Daddy had a great sense of humor.

You must do something similar regarding the painful experiences from your past. Refuse to go back there emotionally; refuse to dredge up negative emotional memories. They will do you no good; in fact, strongly felt negative emotions hold the potential to severely stifle your progress.

Think of it like this: Every person has two main files in his or her memory system. The first is a file filled with all the good things that have happened to us. It's full of our victories and accomplishments, all the things that have brought us joy and happiness through the years.

Refuse to dredge up negative emotional memories.

The second file is just the opposite. It's filled with the hurts and pains of the past, all the negative things that have happened to us. It's full of our defeats and failures, things that brought us sadness and sorrow. Throughout life, we can choose which file we will access. Some people repeatedly return to file number two and relive the painful things that have happened to them. They're always thinking about the times somebody did them wrong, the times they were hurt or suffered awful pain. They practically wear out file number two. They're so preoccupied with the negative things, they never get around to exploring file number one. They hardly think about the good things that have happened to them.

If you want to be free, if you want to overcome self-pity, throw away the key to file number two. Don't go back there anymore. Keep your mind focused on the good things God has done in your life.

✌ Today's Prayer for Your Best Life Now ✌

Thank You, Father, that my past is forgiven, and I can live today fresh and clean because of what You have done for me. Help me to focus on the great future that You have for me.

BAGGAGE DRAGGERS

Scripture Reading for Your Best Life Now   Hebrews 12:1–15

Let us also lay aside every encumbrance and the sin which so easily entangles us, and let us run with endurance the race that is set before us.

Hebrews 12:1 nasb

Many people wonder why they're not happy. Often, it's because they are dragging around all sorts of baggage from the past. Somebody offended them last week, so they have packed that pain in their bag. A month ago they lost their temper, said some things they shouldn't have, and they have that stuffed in their bag, too. Ten years ago, a loved one died and they just don't understand why. They've got that anger and doubt stashed in still another bag. Growing up, they weren't treated right. They've got that suitcase full of junk, too. They've been carrying these heavy bags for years; they are loaded down by their collection of burdens, and then they wonder why they can't live a rich, full life!

Worse yet, they drag their baggage with them everywhere they go. Not only do they hold on to their baggage, but they like to unpack it every once in a while, just to make sure it's all still there. They take some things out and look at them, and relive all that hurt and pain. Then they pack it up again and drag it someplace else!

Marie (not her real name) went through a failed relationship in her marriage many years ago. She prayed that God would bring somebody new into her life. Sure enough, she met a fine gentleman, a very godly, successful man, and she was excited about their friendship. But she made the mistake of dragging all her baggage into that new relationship. When they were together, she talked constantly about all she had been through, how she was emotionally drained, and how mistreated she had been.

God will give you a new beginning.

That gentleman told me later that Marie was so focused on her past, so caught up in what she had been through, he just couldn't deal with it anymore. He finally stopped calling her, and just moved on.

Unfortunately, something like that happens all too often. If you hold on to the hurts and pains of the past, they will poison you wherever you go. You may think that other people are the problem, but I want to encourage you to examine your own heart. Look on the inside, because you may very well find out that *you* are the problem. Maybe you've been a baggage dragger. And you can't drag around baggage from the past and expect to have good, healthy relationships.

God did not create us to carry around all the baggage from the past. In fact, He says, "Lay aside every encumbrance and the sin that so easily entangles us." In other words, let it go. You do not have to live depressed and discouraged because of what you've gone through. Maybe you've been holding on to painful memories or attitudes that have been keeping you bitter, discouraged, emotionally worn out, physically run down, depleted of energy and enthusiasm, and living in self-pity. Sadly, your situation will not change until you put your foot down and make a decision to do something about it. Say, "No, I'm not going to be a prisoner of my past anymore. I have had enough. I'm going to get rid of all this baggage. I'm going to stop focusing on my disappointments. I'm moving on with my life, knowing that God has good things in store." If you'll develop that kind of attitude, God will give you a new beginning. You'll see things improve.

If somebody hurt you, give that to God and He'll pay you back. He will make it up to you. Quit dwelling on your disappointments. Quit mourning over something that's over and done. Don't make the mistake of dragging the pains of yesterday over into today. Stop sitting around feeling sorry for yourself. If you continue to wallow in despair, not only will you stay stuck in the past, but you will sink deeper and deeper.

Friend, God is bigger than your past. He's bigger than your disappointments. He's bigger than your problems. You may have made a lot of mistakes, but God can turn those things all around. People may have hurt you and done you wrong, but if you'll leave it up to God, He'll pay you back. He'll make your wrongs right. Get rid of that baggage and start focusing on your possibilities. Let hope fill your heart. Your future can start today. No matter what you've been through, no matter how difficult it was, God is saying there are great days ahead for you. He still has good things in store.

❧ Today's Prayer for Your Best Life Now ❧

God, I'm dropping my baggage from the past right here. I'm letting go of it and giving it to You. I don't want to drag it along with me any longer. Thank You for taking this heavy load off my heart.

DO YOU WANT TO BE WELL?

I do believe, but help me not to doubt!

MARK 9:24 NLT

THE MAN IN today's Scripture reading had been crippled for thirty-eight years. He spent every day of his life lying on a mat by the pool of Bethesda, hoping for a miracle. One day Jesus saw the man lying there in need. It was obvious that he was crippled, but Jesus asked the man a strange question: "Do you want to be made well?" (John 5:6 NKJV).

The man's response was interesting. He began listing all of his excuses. "I'm all alone. I don't have anyone to help me. Other people have let me down. Other people always seem to get ahead of me. I don't have a chance in life."

Jesus didn't say, "Yes, friend, I agree with you. You've had a tough time."

No, Jesus looked at him and said, in effect, "If you are serious about getting well, if you are serious about getting your life in order, if you really want to get out of this mess, here's what you must do: Get up off the ground, take up your bed, and be on your way." When the man did what Jesus told him to do, he was miraculously healed!

That's a message for us today. If you're serious about being well, if you really want to be made physically and emotionally whole, you must get up and get moving with your life. No more lying around feeling sorry for yourself. Stop making excuses; stop blaming people or circumstances that disappointed you. Instead, start forgiving the people who hurt you. Trust God, get up, and step into the great future He has for you.

Today can be a turning point in your life, a season of new beginnings. Refuse to live with a victim mentality any longer. You might be saying, "I just don't understand why this is happening to me. I don't understand why I got sick. Why did my loved one die? Why did my marriage break apart? Why was I raised in such an abusive environment?"

You may never know the answer. But don't use that as an excuse to wallow in self-pity. Many of the "why" questions of life will remain a conundrum, but trust in God, and accept the fact that there will be some unanswered questions. Keep in mind, just because you don't know the answer doesn't mean that one does not exist. You simply haven't discovered it yet.

Usually, we can deal with a situation if we can locate a file in our thinking in which to put it. But what happens when things don't make sense? When a good person is stricken with a serious illness? Or a child is born with a birth injury? Or a husband or a wife walks out of a marriage? What happens when life doesn't fit neatly into our categories?

Many of the "why" questions of life will remain a conundrum, but trust in God.

Each of us should have what I call an "I Don't Understand It" file. When something comes up for which you have no reasonable answer, instead of dwelling on it and trying to figure it out, simply place it in your "I Don't Understand It" file.

In the meantime, you must muster enough faith to say, "God, I don't understand it, but I trust You. And I'm not going to spend all my time trying to figure out why certain things have happened. I'm going to trust You to make something good out of it. You're a good God, and I know You have my best interests at heart. You promised that all things will work together for my good."

That is faith, and that is the attitude God honors.

When my mother was growing up, she developed the dreaded disease of polio. She had to wear a heavy brace on her leg for many years, and even today, one leg remains shorter than the other. Mother could have easily said, "God, this isn't fair. Why did this happen to me?"

But Mother didn't do that. She refused to see herself as the victim. She saw herself as the victor. And God brought her out of that difficulty. Your difficulties can make you bitter, or they can make you better. They can drag you down and make you a sour person, or they can inspire you to reach for new heights.

You can sit back and make excuses to stay in mediocrity. That's easy. You can make excuses, have a bad attitude, or a poor self-image. Anyone can do that. But if you want to live your best life now, you must reach out to God, shake off self-pity, get up, and move on with your life.

✂ Today's Prayer for Your Best Life Now ✂

Rather than focusing on why certain things happen to me or to those I love, I choose to focus on You, Father, who You are, and what You have promised to do in my life as I trust You. I want to be better; I want to be healed from anything that would keep me locked in the past. Today, I will step into the great future that You have for me.

TRUSTING THROUGH DISAPPOINTMENT

SCRIPTURE READING FOR YOUR BEST LIFE NOW   2 Samuel 12:1–25

Jesus said to her, "I am the resurrection and the life; he who believes in Me will live even if he dies, and everyone who lives and believes in Me will never die. Do you believe this?"

JOHN 11:25–26 NASB

WHEN KING DAVID'S newborn baby was dreadfully sick and near death, David prayed night and day, believing that God could heal his child. He wouldn't eat or drink; he didn't shave or shower. He didn't attend to any business. He wouldn't do anything but pray, crying out to God.

Despite David's passionate prayers, on the seventh day the child died. David's servants worried how they were going to tell the king that his baby was dead. They thought he would be so devastated, so distraught that he couldn't handle it. But when David finally figured out what had happened, he surprised them all. He got up off the floor, washed his face, and put on some fresh clothes. Then he asked his servants to bring him some food, and he sat down and ate a meal.

His servants were confused. They said, "David, when your child was alive, you fasted and prayed. But now that he's gone, you act as though nothing's wrong."

David answered, "Yes, I fasted and prayed when my son was

sick, thinking that God might heal him. But now that he is gone, I cannot bring him back. He will not return to me, but I will go to be with him." Notice David's attitude. He didn't get bitter. He didn't question God. He could have snarled, "God, I thought You loved me. Why didn't You answer my prayers?"

When you go through situations you don't understand, don't become bitter.

David didn't do that. He dared to trust God in the midst of his disappointment. He washed his face and moved on with his life.

Friend, you and I have to learn to do the same thing. People may have mistreated you. Somebody may have walked out on you, or maybe you prayed fervently, yet God didn't answer your prayer the way you had anticipated. That's over and done. You cannot change the past; there's nothing you can do about it now. But you must make a decision. Are you going to relive all those painful memories, or are you going to stay in an attitude of faith?

You must walk out of any emotional bondage in which you have been living. Nobody can do it for you. You must rise up out of those ashes. You must forgive the people who have hurt you. You have to release all those hurts and pains. Leave the past behind. When you go through situations you don't understand, don't become bitter. Don't question God. Learn to do as David did: Just wash your face, keep a good attitude, and move on. Get ready for the new things God has in store for you.

If you will stay in an attitude of faith and victory, God has promised that He will turn those emotional wounds around. He'll use them to your advantage, and you will come out better than you would have had they not happened to you.

⨯⨯ Today's Prayer for Your Best Life Now ⨯⨯

Father, I admit that sometimes I'm more surprised when You do answer my prayers than when You don't. I know that I don't deserve Your kindness, that like David, I've made some bad decisions, done wrong, and deserve nothing. But thank You for loving me even through my mistakes, failures, and wrong choices. Help me, Father, to trust You through my disappointments.

GET TO THE ROOT OF THE MATTER

SCRIPTURE READING FOR YOUR BEST LIFE NOW   1 Timothy 1:5–17

*Look after each other so that none of you will miss out
on the special favor of God. Watch out that no bitter
root of unbelief rises up among you, for whenever it
springs up, many are corrupted by its poison.*

HEBREWS 12:15 NLT

A LOT OF people are trying to improve their lives by dealing with
the external aspects. They are attempting to rectify their bad
habits such as overeating, stress, sleeplessness, or bad tempers.
They're dealing with the fruit of their lives, trying to change those
things, and that is noble. But the truth is, unless they get to the
root, they will never be able to change the fruit. Because as long
as that bitter root is growing on the inside, that problem will per-
sist and keep popping up time and again. You may be able to control your behavior for a while or keep a good attitude for a short
period of time, but have you ever wondered why you can't really
get free? Why can't you overcome that destructive habit?

You have to go deeper. You must discover why you are so
angry, why you can't get along with other people, why you are always so negative. If you'll look deeply and get to the root, then
you'll be able to deal with the problem, overcome it, and truly
begin to change.

In *Your Best Life Now*, I told of a young woman who once

came to my dad for spiritual help. She had been sexually assaulted by several boys years ago, back in her teens. Consequently, she could not have an intimate relationship with her husband. One day she had a dream that reminded her of what had happened when she was a young girl. When she awakened, she realized that she still carried all that anger and hatred in her heart toward those boys. It was buried deep down inside, and it was affecting her relationship with her husband many years later. She knew it wasn't going to be easy, but she recognized she had to deal with that unforgiveness, or she would never have a healthy relationship. She prayed, "God, You know it wasn't fair. You know what they did to me. But I'm not going to hold on to it any longer; I'm not going to allow the pain from the past to poison my present and my future. God, I forgive those boys right now."

Interestingly, from that moment on, she was able to enjoy a healthy relationship with her husband. She couldn't change by dealing with the fruit; she had to get down to the root. And once the bitter root was gone, she was able to break free from her past.

Certainly, you do not need to go back and relive every negative experience, recalling all the painful memories of the past. Not at all. But you should examine your heart to make sure you haven't buried anger and unforgiveness on the inside. If you have areas in your life where you are constantly struggling, trying to change but finding yourself unable to do so, ask God to show you what's keeping you from

Once the bitter root was gone, she was able to break free from her past.

being free. Ask God to show you if you have any bitter roots that need to be dug up and extracted. If God brings something to light, be quick to deal with it. Be willing to change. Don't let the poisons of the past continue to contaminate your life.

⬖ Today's Prayer for Your Best Life Now ⬖

Father, I don't want roots of bitterness from my past or any other destructive, poisonous roots to be growing beneath the surface in my life. Please reveal any foul thoughts, words, attitudes, or actions that might contaminate my relationship with You, and with others.

FORGIVE AND MOVE ON

Be kind to one another, tender-hearted, forgiving each
other, just as God in Christ also has forgiven you.

                            EPHESIANS 4:32 NASB

To LIVE IN the present moment, making the most of this day, we must forgive those people who have hurt us in the past. Too often, we try to collect our debts from other people. When somebody hurts us, we feel like they owe us. Somebody should pay for that pain we have suffered! That's what happens when you're trapped in the past. You're always trying to collect those debts. You'll take it out on other people even though they weren't involved.

Victoria and I have met some women who can't have a good relationship with a man because they were mistreated by the men in their lives as they were growing up. Now, every time they get into a new relationship, they try to make that new man pay them back for the old injustices inflicted by someone else. They're trying to collect a debt they feel is owed to them.

But here's the problem: Only God can pay that debt; other people can't do it. Moreover, you should not drag something that happened in the past into your relationships today. Don't punish your spouse, your children, your friends, or your coworkers for something that happened to you when you were growing up. Instead, turn it over to God. Keep your heart free from bitterness and resentment, and don't try to collect a debt that only God can pay.

Start each day afresh and anew, especially in your family relationships. Don't let little things build up. Don't harbor unforgiveness and resentment. Don't allow the attitude, *Well, she's not treating me nicely today, so I'm not going to talk to her.* Or, *He's not being very kind; I'm going to give him the cold shoulder.*

Keep your heart free and clean.

Such vengeful snubs may seem insignificant to you, but over time if you're not careful, that bitter attitude will build, and it'll end up causing you major problems. You've got to do your best to keep your own heart free and clean, because if you're poisoned with unforgiveness, bitterness, or resentment on the inside, eventually it will show up on the outside. You cannot keep it buried. It will come out and begin to affect your personality. You'll be hard to get along with, easily offended, uptight, and negative.

That's why the Scripture instructs us to put on a fresh new attitude every morning. Each morning, forgive the people who have hurt you. Every morning, let go of your disappointments and setbacks. Each new morning, receive God's mercy and forgiveness for the mistakes you've made, and forgive others for the hurts they have inflicted on you. Today focus on your possibilities; focus on what you can change rather than what you cannot change.

What's done is done. If somebody offended, disappointed, or mistreated you yesterday, either you can get bitter or you can forgive them and move on. Remember, if you refuse to forgive others, God will not forgive you.

If you lost your temper yesterday, quit dwelling on it. You cannot undo that. You need to ask for forgiveness and then do better today.

Was your boss rude to you and jumped down your throat? Let

it go. Don't go to work tomorrow with a chip on your shoulder. It's a new day.

You didn't get that promotion you were hoping for? Okay, God must have something better in store for you. Move on, knowing that all things are going to work together for your good.

I'm not implying that you should take the easy way out and not be responsible for your words or actions. If you have done wrong, offended someone or hurt somebody, you should seek that person's forgiveness. But if you're trying to fix something that you know there's no way to fix, and you've done everything you can do, you must simply leave that up to God. Receive His mercy and go out to live your best life now.

❧ Today's Prayer for Your Best Life Now ❧

Father, I dare to forgive others, because I know You have forgiven me. Help me each day to be tenderhearted, to forgive those people who have hurt me, used me, or otherwise brought pain into my life.

GET RID OF THE POISON

SCRIPTURE READING FOR YOUR BEST LIFE NOW   Psalm 95:1–11

Search me, O God, and know my heart; try me and know my anxious thoughts; and see if there be any hurtful way in me, and lead me in the everlasting way.
                                        PSALM 139:23–24 NASB

YEARS AGO IN a remote part of Africa, people were dying because their water supply was contaminated. Even health experts were puzzled since the village got its water supply from a fresh mountain stream that was fed from a spring. When the experts sent some divers down to search the spring's opening, they were shocked at what they discovered. A large mother pig and her baby piglets evidently had drowned and somehow gotten stuck there, contaminating the crystal clear, pure mountain spring water. The divers removed the dead pigs, and the water began to flow clean and pure once again.

Something similar sometimes takes place in our lives. We've all had negative things happen to us. Maybe last week, last month, or ten years ago somebody hurt us. And too often, instead of letting it go and giving it to God, we've held on to it. We haven't forgiven, and just as those pigs soured that crystal clear water, our own lives have become contaminated. The root of bitterness has taken hold.

Worse yet, after a while, we accept it. We make room in our hearts for that bitterness; we learn to live with it. "Well, I'm just an angry person. That's just my personality. I'm always like this. I'm always bitter. This is who I am."

No, with all due respect, that's not who you are. You need to get rid of the poison that is polluting your life. You were made to be a crystal clear stream. God created you in His image. He wants you to be happy, healthy, and whole. God wants you to enjoy life to the full, not to live with bitterness and resentment, polluted and putrefied yourself and contaminating everyone else with whom you have influence.

Imagine yourself as a crystal clear stream. It doesn't matter how polluted the stream may be right now, or how muddy or murky the waters may look in your life today. If you'll begin to forgive the people who have offended you, and release all those hurts and pains, that bitterness will leave and you'll begin to see that crystal clear water once again. You'll begin to experience the joy, peace, and freedom God intended you to have.

Maybe that's why David said, "Search my heart, oh God, and point out anything in me that makes You sad" (see Psalm 139:23–24). We need to search our hearts and make sure we haven't let any roots of bitterness take hold.

It may not be a big thing that is polluting your stream. Maybe your spouse is not spending as much time with you as you'd like, and you can feel yourself starting to get resentful. You're short with your mate, sarcastic, cryptic, or unfriendly. You're intentionally becoming harder to get along with.

> The longer we hold on to resentment, the deeper that root of bitterness grows.

Watch out! That root of bitterness will contaminate your life. Keep your stream pure. Don't let your heart get polluted. The Bible talks about being quick to forgive, and the longer we wait, the harder it's going to be. The longer we hold on to resentment, the deeper that root of bitterness grows.

Sometimes, instead of forgiving quickly, letting go of the hurts and pains of the past, we quietly bury them deep down inside our hearts and minds. We don't want to talk about the issue. We don't want to think about it. We want to ignore it and hope that it will go away.

It won't. Just like those pigs trapped beneath the water, one day that contamination will show up in your life, and it will be a mess. It will cause you even more pain and sorrow, and if you refuse to deal with it, that bitterness could kill you.

Deal with it today by forgiving anyone who has hurt you, and then choose to live today in freedom and freshness. As you do, the joy of the Lord will burst forth within you like a fresh mountain spring.

✂ Today's Prayer for Your Best Life Now ✂

Father, I want the streams of my life to flow with pure, clean water. Please search my heart, O God, and help me to detect anything profane or unwelcome in heaven. Give me the courage to make the changes You are calling me to make.

START CLEAN EACH DAY

SCRIPTURE READING FOR YOUR BEST LIFE NOW   Psalm 5:1–12

*My voice shalt thou hear in the morning, O LORD; in
the morning will I direct my prayer unto thee, and will
look up.*

PSALM 5:3 KJV

OUR TIME HERE on this earth is so short. What a shame it would
be to allow something that happened in the past—whether it was
twenty years ago or twenty minutes ago—to ruin the rest of this
day.

I've made up my mind to do my best to enjoy every single day.
I may make mistakes; things may not always go my way. I may be
disappointed at times, but I've made a decision that I'm going to
live my life happy anyway. I'm not going to allow what does or
doesn't happen to me to steal my joy and keep me from God's
abundant life.

Sometimes we allow something that happens early in the morning to disrupt our entire day. Say that you got stuck in a traffic
jam, causing you to be an hour late for work, which throws your
schedule off a bit. What can you do about it? You can either let
that inconvenience frustrate you and ruin the rest of your day, or
you can let it go and be happy anyway. After all, you can't do anything about it. No matter how upset you get, you can't undo it.

You might as well enjoy the day knowing that God is still in control.

Or, maybe somebody offends you at ten o'clock in the morning. They're rude to you, and now it is ten-thirty. Your attitude should be, *I'm moving on. I'm not holding on to that offense. That's over and done. I'm not going to let it sour the rest of my day. No, I'm traveling light; I'm not going to carry any extra burdens. I'm going to keep my heart pure and I'm going to live happily.*

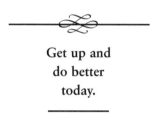

Get up and do better today.

Maybe at one o'clock you find out that you didn't get that big sales contract you had worked on so hard. Now it's two o'clock. Your attitude should be, *That's not going to ruin the rest of my week. Yes, I'm disappointed. Yes, I would have loved to have it, but I know complaining isn't going to change anything. I'm going to keep a smile on my face and remain in an attitude of faith. I know God must have something better in store.*

When you get up in the morning, you may recall all the mistakes you made yesterday. You can probably list a complete inventory of everything you did wrong, the times you blew it, when you had a bad attitude, or when you were undisciplined. "Well, I should have read my Bible more yesterday. I really didn't pray enough. I wanted to clean the house, but I just watched TV instead. I don't know why I'm so undisciplined."

No, don't start your day off like that. Get up in the morning and say, "Father, I thank You that this is going to be a great day. I thank You that I have discipline, self-control; that I make good decisions. I may not have done what I could have yesterday, but that day's gone. I'm going to get up and do better today."

If you blew your diet yesterday, quit thinking about it. That day's over. Get up and do better today. If you heap guilt on yourself, you'll make excuses, and you'll go out and eat fourteen gallons of ice cream today! Let it go.

Maybe you were short-tempered with one of your employees last week. Let it go and do better next week.

Maybe you spent too much money last week. Let it go and do better this week.

Any morning you get up feeling guilty about yesterday, if you fail to correct it right then and there, that day's going to be ruined as well. You'll drag around depressed and defeated. Don't fall into that trap.

Instead, get up every morning and receive God's love and mercy. When you make mistakes, don't beat yourself up over them. Nobody is perfect. You simply need to ask God for forgiveness and then move on, confident that the moment you ask, God forgives you.

God does not want you to mope around defeated. He wants you to get up and move on. Not only does God forgive you, but He chooses not to remember your mistakes. If somebody keeps bringing up negative incidents from your past, you know that's not God. You may have done some things you're not proud of, but when you asked God to forgive you, He washed those things away. Furthermore, He doesn't even keep a record of it. He's not going to flip back through His files one day and say, "Oh, wait a minute. I found something on your record back there in 2005. I can't bless you."

No, as far as God is concerned, you don't even have a past. It's forgiven and gone. You are ready for a great present and a bright future. God let go of the past. The question is: Will you let it go? Will you quit remembering what God has chosen to forget?

∞ Today's Prayer for Your Best Life Now ∞

Yes, Father, I accept Your forgiveness. Thank You for loving me even when I make mistakes, poor choices, or wrong decisions. Help me to live today free of the past.

THE GOD OF ANOTHER CHANCE

SCRIPTURE READING FOR YOUR BEST LIFE NOW   Romans 8:28–39

If we confess our sins, He is faithful and righteous to forgive us our sins and to cleanse us from all unrighteousness.

1 JOHN 1:9 NASB

WE ALL MAKE mistakes, but God does not disqualify us simply because we have failed. He's the God of another chance. You may have missed plan A for your life, but God has a plan B, a plan C, a plan D, and a plan E. God will always find a way to get you to your final destination if you will trust Him.

The Old Testament records how King David ordered a man murdered so he could marry his wife. But when David repented, God forgave him and still used him in a great way.

A man named Saul hated Christians; he chased them down, persecuted them, and had them thrown in jail. Yet God forgave him, changed his name to Paul, and he ended up writing more than half the New Testament.

Rahab was a prostitute, yet God used her to help deliver the children of Israel. Nobody is too far gone, no matter what he's done. You need to know that God still loves you. He has a great plan for your life; He has not run out of mercy. If you have asked His forgiveness, God has already forgiven you. The question is: Will you forgive yourself? Will you quit living in guilt and condemnation? Will you let the past be the past and live today in an attitude of faith and victory?

That is what my father had to do. Daddy went through a tragedy early in his life. He married quite young, and unfortunately that wasn't one of his better choices. Sadly, the marriage didn't work out, and he went through a divorce. Daddy was heartbroken. His dreams were shattered, and he didn't think he would ever preach again. It was one of the darkest hours of Daddy's life. He was tempted to hold on to the hurt and pain, continually blaming himself. He could have easily allowed his disappointment and disillusionment to keep him from moving forward and fulfilling his God-given destiny.

But Daddy had to quit mourning over what he had lost; he had to learn how to receive God's mercy, and to start believing God for something better.

Maybe you've made some serious mistakes; you've done some things that weren't the best for your life, and now you're living in guilt, condemnation, or with a sense of disqualification. You will remain trapped in those doldrums unless you learn how to receive God's mercy and forgiveness, and move on with your life.

Receive
God's mercy
and
forgiveness,
and move on
with your
life.

That is what my father did. Daddy made a decision to receive God's mercy for his mistakes and failures. And little by little God began to restore Daddy's life and his ministry. Daddy began to minister again, but he never dreamed he'd get married again and have another family.

Then one day he met a nurse working at one of the hospitals where he visited some of his church members when they were sick. For my dad, it was love at first sight. He started looking for any reason he could find to stop by that hospital. I mean, he would visit your great-aunt's third cousin's next-door neighbor if you asked him! He was there so much, my mother told one of her friends, "That minister has the sickest congregation I've ever seen!" She didn't realize at the time that Daddy was there to see *her*. To make a long story short, they fell in love and got married. God gave Daddy beauty for his ashes, and Daddy went on to touch the world.

He pastored Lakewood Church in Houston for more than forty years, and today all five of my parents' children are working in the ministry. God took what the enemy meant for evil, and He turned it around and used it for good. But I don't believe that would have happened if Daddy had stayed trapped in the past, focused on his sadness and disappointments. I don't believe it ever would have happened if Daddy had not learned how to receive God's mercy.

Are you living in guilt and condemnation because of your past mistakes? Let all that go. You can't do anything about the past, but you can do something about right now. If you've made mistakes, ask for forgiveness and then move on. God still has a great future for you.

❧ Today's Prayer for Your Best Life Now ❧

Father, today I receive Your mercy and forgiveness. Despite my past, I believe You still have great things in store for me. Teach me how to shake off disappointment, guilt, or condemnation and live today in an attitude of faith.

EVICT THAT VICTIM MENTALITY

SCRIPTURE READING FOR YOUR BEST LIFE NOW   1 Kings 19:1–21

Arise, shine; for your light has come, and the glory of the LORD has risen upon you.

ISAIAH 60:1 NASB

TOO MANY PEOPLE nowadays are living with a victim mentality. They are so focused on what they've been through, complaining about how unfair it was, they don't realize they are dragging the pains of the past into the present. It's almost as though they get up each day and fill a big wheelbarrow with junk from the past and bring it into the new day.

Let go of that stuff! Your past does not have to poison your future. Just because you've been through some hurt and pain, or perhaps one or more of your dreams have been shattered, that doesn't mean God doesn't have another plan. God still has a bright future in store for you. But you must understand this basic principal: *The past is the past.* You cannot undo anything that's happened to you. You can't relive one moment in the past. But you can do something about right now. Your attitude should be, *I refuse to dwell on the negative things that have happened to me. I'm not going to think about all that I've lost. I'm not going to focus on what could have been or should have been. No, I'm going to draw the line in the sand. This is a new day, and I'm going to start moving forward, knowing that God has a bright fu-*

ture in store for me. If you do that, God will give you a new beginning.

In the Old Testament, when the people were going through mourning or some kind of loss, they marked their foreheads with ashes to signify their sorrow. This type of mourning was permissible and expected. Interestingly, God's people were allowed to grieve for a certain period of time, then God told them to get up and get going with their lives.

It's the same way with us. When we go through some sort of loss or disappointment, God doesn't expect us to be emotionless. It's okay to go through a time of grieving. But don't allow yourself to live there. Don't let that season of mourning turn into a lifestyle of mourning, living a sour and negative life, going around with a chip on your shoulder. When we do that, we're holding on to the ashes.

In the Bible, a good man named Job had all sorts of terrible things happen to him. He lost his family, his health, and his business. Not surprisingly, in the midst of that mess, Job didn't make good choices—at least, not at first. In fact, Job sat down among the ashes (see Job 2:8).

Many people are doing the same thing today. They've been through tough times. Things haven't gone their way. And instead of shaking off those disappointments, they sit down in the ashes of defeat, never expecting anything good.

Are you sitting in some ashes today? Are you still sour because you didn't get that promotion a couple of years ago? Is your attitude negative because you weren't able to buy that house or car you really wanted? Are you bitter because a relationship didn't work out, or angry because you were treated abusively as you were growing up?

Quit mourning over something that's already over and done. You've got to shake yourself out of that *victim* mentality and start having a *victor* mentality. This is a new day. Your future can start right now. It doesn't matter what you've been through, or how somebody has treated you; God wants to turn all that around.

You need to get a new fire. Nobody can do this for you. I can encourage you. Your friends can cheer you on. But it's not going to do any good until you put your foot down and make a decision that you will no longer live as a prisoner to your past.

Say something like this: "I may have been mistreated; I may have gotten the short end of the stick, but I'm not going to sit around in self-pity. I'm going to keep a smile on my face and hold my head high. I know God's going to make it up to me. I know God will bring joy for my mourning." Develop that victor mentality. Let hope fill your heart, then things will begin to improve.

Many people give up too easily, sitting in the ashes of defeat, mourning over what they've been through, bitter because a dream didn't work out, angry because their loved one didn't get healed. I talked to a young woman recently who was so sour because her parents couldn't send her to college. She thought she was going to get a scholarship, but it all fell through. Then she couldn't get the finances she needed to attend school. Now she was working at a job she didn't like. As she was telling me her story, I could feel the poison coming out of her. She was so bitter and negative, it was destroying her future. I told her, "You've got to let all that go before anything's going to change. You've got to quit thinking about it, quit talking about it, quit rehearsing it all the time. All that's doing is keeping you negative and sour. There's nothing the enemy would love to do any more than to deceive you into sitting in the ashes of defeat your whole lifetime."

God still has a bright future for you.

If you've made that mistake, the good news is, you don't have to stay there. Today can be a turning point. God still has a bright future for you. He wants to take those negative experiences and use them to your advantage, if you'll dare to do your part and rise up out of those ashes.

When you get up each morning, shake off the ashes of yesterday's discouragements and disappointments. Let your attitude be, *I'm forgetting what lies behind and I'm pressing forward*. In other words, "I'm throwing away my rearview mirror. I'm not looking back anymore. I'm not looking to the left or to the right. I'm looking straight ahead. I'm pressing forward, knowing God has good things in store for me."

If you will do that, God will give you joy for your mourning.

✤ Today's Prayer for Your Best Life Now ✤

I know the ashes signify that which has been destroyed in my life, Father, but beginning this moment, I believe You can bring new fire into my life. I refuse to dwell on my disappointments. Instead, I will trust You for new appointments.

FORGIVE FOR YOUR OWN SAKE

*He that covereth his sins shall not prosper: but whoso
confesseth and forsaketh them shall have mercy.*
PROVERBS 28:13 KJV

A FEW DECADES ago, several American companies authorized by
the U.S. government attempted to bury toxic-waste products un-
derground. They filled large metal containers with chemical waste
and other life-threatening products, sealed the drums tightly, and
buried them deep down below the topsoil. They thought that was
the end of it. Within a short time, however, many of the containers began to leak and the toxic waste started seeping to the surface, causing all sorts of problems. In some locations, it killed off
the vegetation and ruined the water supply. People had to move
out of their homes. What went wrong? They tried to bury something that was too toxic. They never dreamed that the materials
they were attempting to bury were so powerful that they were too
toxic for the containers to hold. They never dreamed that one day
those contaminants would resurface, and they would have to deal
with the problem all over again. But this time, the toxic materials
would be dispersed and much more difficult to deal with. Had
they disposed of them properly in the first place, they wouldn't
have had this terrible problem.

It's the same with us. When somebody hurts us, somebody does us wrong, instead of letting it go and trusting God to make it up to us, we bury it deep down inside. We attempt to cram unforgiveness, resentment, anger, and other destructive responses into our "leakproof" containers. We seal those lids tightly, but unfortunately, just as that toxic waste tends to resurface, one day the things you have tamped into your subconscious or buried deeply in the recesses of your heart will rise to the surface and begin to contaminate your life. We can't live with poison inside us and not expect it to eventually do us harm.

> We can't live with poison inside us and not expect it to eventually do us harm.

Forgiveness is the key to being free from toxic bitterness. Forgive the people who hurt you. Forgive the boss who did you wrong. Forgive the friend who betrayed you. Forgive the parent who mistreated you when you were younger. Don't let the root of bitterness grow deeper and continue to contaminate your life.

What does this toxic waste look like in our lives? For some people, it seeps out as anger. In other people, it smells like depression. For others, it reeks of low self-esteem. It can show up in many different ways, sometimes doing damage before we even realize it has reappeared.

You can have success on the outside, but if you're bitter on the inside, it's going to spoil and taint every victory. You must deal with the inside first, then you can really be happy. Then you can experience true, untainted, unalloyed victory in your life.

You may be thinking, *Joel, I can't do it. It's too hard. I just can't forgive. They hurt me too badly.*

Wait a minute! You are not forgiving for *their* sake, you are forgiving for your sake. You are forgiving so that poison doesn't continue to contaminate your life. If somebody has done you a great wrong, don't allow them to continue to hurt you by hanging on to it. You're not hurting them at all. You're hurting yourself.

⁂ Today's Prayer for Your Best Life Now ⁂

Father, I know that when I forgive those who hurt me, it pleases You. Please help me to recognize that forgiveness of others is in my best interest, as well.

TEAR DOWN THE WALLS

SCRIPTURE READING FOR YOUR BEST LIFE NOW   Matthew 18:21–35

If you forgive others for their transgressions, your heavenly Father will also forgive you. But if you do not forgive others, then your Father will not forgive your transgressions.

MATTHEW 6:14–15 NASB

WHEN YOU FORGIVE someone who has hurt or offended you, it is not simply about the other person; you're doing it for your own good, as well. When you hold on to unforgiveness and live with grudges in your heart, you are building walls of separation. You may think that you are protecting yourself, but you aren't. You are simply shutting other people out of your life. You become isolated, alone, warped and imprisoned by your own bitterness. Those walls aren't merely keeping people out; those walls are keeping you penned in.

Do you realize that those walls will also prevent God's blessings from pouring into your life? Those walls can stop up the flow of God's favor. The walls of unforgiveness will keep your prayers from being answered. They'll keep your dreams from coming to pass. You must tear down the walls. You must forgive the people who hurt you so you can get out of prison. You'll never be free until you do. Get that bitterness out of your life. That's the only way you're going to truly be free. You will be amazed at what can happen in your life when you release all that poison.

I told a story in *Your Best Life Now* about a man who attended our church when I was growing up. His hands were so crippled with arthritis, he could hardly use them. But one day he heard my father preaching about unforgiveness, and how it keeps God's power from operating in our lives and prevents our prayers from being answered. He began asking God to help him get rid of anger and resentment in his heart toward those people who had hurt him over the years. As he forgave, the most amazing thing began to happen. One by one, his fingers straightened, and eventually, God restored his hands to normal.

You, too, will be amazed at the great things that start happening in your life when you rid yourself of bitterness and resentment. You may experience genuine physical and emotional healing as you search your heart and are willing to forgive. You may see God's favor in a fresh, new way. You may see your prayers answered more quickly as you let go of the past and get rid of all that poison you now harbor.

When my mother discovered that she was sick with cancer in 1981, one of the first things she did was to make sure she didn't have any unforgiveness in her heart. She sat down and wrote letters to her friends and family, asking us to forgive her if she had ever done any wrong toward us. She wanted to make sure that nothing she was doing or had done would interfere with God's healing power flowing into her.

Unforgiveness keeps God's power from operating in our lives.

Today, you are at a crossroads in your life. You may have issues to deal with or people you need to forgive. You can go one of two ways. You can ignore what you know to be true and keep burying that bitterness in your life, pushing it deeper and allowing it to poison and contaminate you and those around you. Or, you can make a much better choice by getting it out in the open and asking God to help you to totally forgive and let it all go.

✌ Today's Prayer for Your Best Life Now ✌

Father, I don't want to harbor any unforgiveness in my heart. Please shine the searchlight of Your Holy Spirit on every nook and cranny of my being, and let me see the areas where anything evil may be trying to gain a foothold through my own hesitancy to forgive.

DOING RIGHT WHEN IT HURTS

The LORD will vindicate His people, and will have compassion on His servants.

DEUTERONOMY 32:36 NASB

A FEW YEARS ago, somebody dealt unethically with Victoria and me in a business deal. This person didn't keep his end of the bargain, and ended up cheating us out of a lot of money. Victoria and I were tempted to want to pay him back and make his life miserable. After all, he made us suffer; why not make him suffer? It was difficult, but we had to force ourselves to do the right thing, which was to turn the matter over to God.

We said, "God, You know we're being mistreated. You know that what this man is doing is wrong. But God, we're not going to try to get even. We're not going to try to avenge ourselves. We're counting on You to make it up to us."

This process continued for several years, and we didn't see any change. We had to keep reminding ourselves that God is a God of justice. *God is going to pay us back for doing the right thing. God is going to settle our case.*

One day, out of the clear blue, God supernaturally stepped in and turned that situation around. He not only moved that man out of our lives, but He paid us back in abundance for everything he had taken. Sadly, the man who tried to cheat us eventually lost his family, his business, his reputation—everything. And I certainly don't wish that on anybody, but that, too, is the justice of God. You cannot go around continually doing wrong, cheating people and sowing bad seeds, and not expect it to eventually catch up to you. We will reap what we've sown.

Keep doing the right thing.

The Scripture says, "Never avenge yourselves, but leave the way open for [God's] wrath" (Romans 12:19 AMP). Notice, if you try to pay people back, you are closing the door for God to do it. Either you can do it God's way, or you can do it your way. If you're going to let God handle it, you can't have the attitude of: *I'm going to show them what I'm made of.* That will prevent God from avenging you His way. If you want to keep that door open so God can bring true justice into your life, you have to totally turn it over to Him.

Maybe you've been working through a situation and you've been doing the right thing for a long time. Perhaps this has been going on month after month, maybe year after year, and now you're wondering, *Is God ever going to change this situation? Is God ever going to bring about justice? Does He even care about what I'm going through?*

Don't give up! Keep doing the right thing. God is building character in you, and you are passing that test. Remember, the greater the struggle, the greater the reward. The Scripture says, "Don't get tired of doing what's right, for in due season you shall reap if you don't faint" (see Galatians 6:9). Don't grow weary; trust God to bring justice in His timing, not yours.

When David was just a young man, he was anointed by the prophet Samuel to be the next king of Israel. Not long after that, he defeated the giant Goliath, and he became an instant hero throughout the land. People loved him, and his popularity ratings soared off the charts. But King Saul, Israel's ruler at the time, became extremely jealous of David and started doing all sorts of unfair things to David. He had to flee to the mountains, living on the run, going from cave to cave, month after month.

Ironically, David hadn't done anything wrong. He had treated Saul with respect and honor, yet Saul turned around and paid him back by attempting to kill him. David could easily have gotten bitter. He could have said, "God, I thought You chose me to be king. What's going on here?"

But David didn't do that. He kept a good attitude, refusing to hurt Saul, even when he had the opportunity. Although Saul wasn't treating him right, David still respected Saul's position of authority. It's easy to respect those in positions of authority as long as they are being kind to us or when we agree with them. But the true test comes when you get a "Saul" in your life, when somebody treats you unfairly for no apparent reason. If you will keep the right attitude, God will promote you at the proper time.

☙ Today's Prayer for Your Best Life Now ☙

Father, I am trusting You to turn the negative situations in my life for good. I refuse to try to get even, and I will not allow myself to remain discouraged because of how someone else is treating me. With Your help, I will return good for evil, and love in the face of oppression, hatred, or indifference.

KEEP TRUSTING

*Thou wilt keep him in perfect peace, whose mind is
stayed on thee: because he trusteth in thee.*

ISAIAH 26:3 KJV

ALL OF US face disappointments from time to time. No matter
how much faith you have or how good a person you are, sooner
or later, something (or somebody!) will shake your faith to its
foundations. It may be something simple, such as not getting that
promotion you really hoped for; not closing the big sale that you
worked on so hard; not qualifying for a loan to buy that house
you really wanted. Or, it may be something more serious—a marriage relationship falling apart, the death of a loved one, or an in-
curable, debilitating illness. Whatever it is, that disappointment
possesses the potential to derail you and wreck your faith. That's
why it is vital that you recognize in advance that disappointments
will come, and that you learn how to stay on track and deal with
them when they do.

Often, defeating disappointments and letting go of the past are
flip sides of the same coin, especially when you are disappointed
in yourself. When you do something wrong, don't hold on to it
and beat yourself up about it. Admit it, seek forgiveness, and
move on. Be quick to let go of your mistakes and failures, hurts,
pains, and sins.

The disappointments that disturb us the most, however, are usually those caused by other people. Many individuals who have been hurt by others are missing out on their new beginnings because they keep reopening old wounds. But no matter what we have gone through, no matter how unfair it was, or how disappointed we were, we must release it and let it go.

Somebody may have walked out on you. Somebody may have done you a great wrong. You may have prayed fervently for a loved one's life to be saved, yet your loved one died. Leave that with God and go on with your life. The Bible says, "The secret things belong to the LORD" (Deuteronomy 29:29 NASB). Leave them there.

Disappointments almost always accompany setbacks. When you suffer loss, nobody expects you to be an impenetrable rock or an inaccessible island in the sea. Not even God expects you to be so tough that you simply ignore the disappointments in life, shrugging them off as though you are impervious to pain. No, when we experience failure or loss, it's natural to feel remorse or sorrow. That's the way God made us. If you lose your job, most likely you are going to experience a strong sense of disappointment. If you go through a broken relationship, that's going to hurt. If you lose a loved one, there's a time of grieving, a time of sorrow. That is normal and to be expected.

No matter what we have gone through, we must release it and let it go.

But if you are still grieving and feeling sorrow over a disappointment that took place a year or more ago, something is wrong! You are hindering your future. You must make a decision that you are going to move on. It won't happen automatically. You will have to rise up and say, "I don't care how hard this is, I am not going to let this get the best of me."

The enemy loves to deceive us into wallowing in self-pity, fretting, feeling sorry for ourselves, or having a chip on our shoulders. "Why did this happen to me?" "God must not love me. He doesn't answer my prayers." "Why did my marriage end in divorce?" "Why did my business not succeed?" "Why did I lose my loved one?" "Why didn't things work out in my life?"

Such questions may be valid and may even be helpful to consider for a season, but after that, quit wasting your time trying to figure out something you can't change. It's time to move on and start living your best life now.

❧ Today's Prayer for Your Best Life Now ❧

I know that I cannot change a single thing about the past, but I can choose how I will live in the future. Help me to build my faith, Father, to believe that You will bring good even out of those circumstances I don't understand. I choose to trust You for good things in the days ahead.

GOD HAS ANOTHER PLAN

SCRIPTURE READING FOR YOUR BEST LIFE NOW   1 Samuel 16:1–12

Thus says the LORD, "Restrain your voice from weeping and your eyes from tears; for your work shall be rewarded," declares the LORD, "and they will return from the land of the enemy. There is hope for your future," declares the LORD.

JEREMIAH 31:16–17 NASB

SOMETIMES, NO MATTER how hard we pray or how long we stand in faith, things don't turn out as we had hoped. Some are praying for their marriages to be restored; others are asking God to heal a business situation or a rift between coworkers. I encourage people to persevere, to continue praying and believing for good things to happen. But we must also understand that God will not change another person's will. He has given every human being free will to choose which way he or she will go, whether to do right or wrong.

You may be heartbroken over a failed relationship or a bankrupt business, but you do not need to stay heartbroken. Don't carry around all that hurt and pain year after year. Don't let rejection fester inside you. God has something new in store for you.

When God allows one door to close, He will open another door for you, revealing something bigger and better. The Bible says that God will take the evil the enemy brings into our lives, and if we'll

keep the right attitude, He'll turn it around and use it for our good
(see Genesis 50:20). He wants to take those disappointments and
turn them into reappointments. But understand, whether you will
experience all those good things in your future depends to a large
extent on your willingness to let go of
the past.

**God desires
your
restoration
even more
than you do!**

Never put a question mark where
God has put a period. Avoid the tendency to dwell on what you could have
done, which career you should have
pursued, or that person you wish you
would have married. Quit living in a
negative frame of mind, stewing about
something that is over and done. Focus on what you *can* change,
rather than what you cannot. Shake yourself out of that "should
have, could have, would have" mentality, and don't let the regrets
of yesterday destroy the hopes and dreams of tomorrow.

You can't do anything about what's gone, but you can do a
great deal about what remains. You may have made some poor
choices that have caused you awful heartache and pain. Perhaps
you feel that you have blown it, that your life is in shambles and
beyond repair. You may feel disqualified from God's best, convinced that you must settle for second best the rest of your life because of the poor decisions you made.

Worse yet, maybe you weren't the person who made the bad
choices, but somebody else's foolish decisions caused you to experience wrenching heartache and pain. Regardless, you must stop
dwelling on it. Let the past be the past. Forgive the person who
caused you the trouble and start clean right where you are today.
If you continue to dwell on those past disappointments, you will
block God's blessings in your life today. It's simply not worth it.
Beyond that, God desires your restoration even more than you do!

The prophet Samuel suffered a horrible disappointment in his
relationship with the first king of Israel, a man named Saul. As a

young man, Saul was humble and shy. Then, at God's direction, Samuel picked him out of the crowd and declared him to be the king of Israel. Samuel did his best to help Saul be a king who was pleasing unto God.

Unfortunately, Saul refused to live in obedience to God, and God eventually rejected him as the king. Imagine how Samuel must have felt. Maybe you've invested a lot of time, effort, money, emotion, and energy in a relationship; you did your best to make it work out. But for some reason, things got off course, and now you feel as though you have been robbed.

That's how Samuel must have felt. Devastated. Heartbroken. Disappointed. But as Samuel was nursing his wounded heart, God asked him an important question: "Samuel, how long are you going to mourn over Saul?" (see 1 Samuel 16:1). Perhaps God is asking you a similar question today: "How long are you going to mourn over that failed relationship?" "How long are you going to mourn over your broken dreams?" That's the problem with excessive mourning. When we focus on our disappointments, we stop God from bringing fresh new blessings into our lives.

God went on to tell Samuel, "Fill up your horn with oil and be on your way. I'm sending you to the house of Jesse, for I have chosen one of his sons to be the new king." In other words, God said, "Samuel, if you will quit mourning and get going, I'll show you a new, better beginning."

Yes, Saul was God's first choice, but when Saul wouldn't walk in obedience, God didn't say, "Well, Samuel, I'm so sorry. Saul blew it, and that ruins everything." No, God always can come up with another plan. Notice what God told Samuel to do: *Fill your horn with oil.* Have a fresh new attitude. Put a smile on your face. Get the spring back in your step and be on your way.

Samuel could have said, "God, I just can't do this. I'm too heartbroken. I gave so much of myself in that relationship and now it's gone, wasted."

But if Samuel would not have trusted God at that point, he

might have missed King David, one of the greatest kings in the Bible. Similarly, if we wallow in our disappointments, we risk missing out on the new things God wants to do in our lives. It's time to get up and get going. God has another plan for you. And it is better than you can imagine!

✻ Today's Prayer for Your Best Life Now ✻

Although I've been disappointed by other people and events in the past, Father, I am going to keep expecting blessings and good things in the future, because of You.

BEAUTY FOR ASHES

The Spirit of the Lord GOD is upon Me, because the LORD has anointed Me to preach good tidings to the poor; He has sent Me to heal the brokenhearted . . . to console those who mourn in Zion, to give them beauty for ashes, the oil of joy for mourning, the garment of praise for the spirit of heaviness.

ISAIAH 61:1–3 NKJV

MANY INDIVIDUALS SPEND their lives looking in their rearview mirrors thinking about what could have been, what should have been, always dwelling on the pains of yesterday. If you've had unfair things happen to you—maybe you lost a job, or you were mistreated, or a spouse was unfaithful—you must make a decision today that you're going to let all that go. If you carry it around with you, soon you will develop a victim mentality that will interfere with God's doing good things in your life.

The Scripture says that God wants to give us beauty for our ashes, joy for our mourning, rejoicing for our heaviness. But here's the key: You have to let go of the ashes before God can give you the beauty. Ashes represent what's left over after something's been burned up. In other words, they represent our broken dreams, our disappointments, our hurts, our failures. We all have our share of ashes, and God wants to give us beauty in exchange for them. But you cannot hold on to the ashes and have the beauty at the same time. You must let go of your shattered dreams if you want God to give you fresh, new dreams. Quit dwelling on your disappointments. Forgive the people who have hurt you. Release any remaining bitterness, and then God will give you beauty; He will give you a new beginning.

"But Joel, those people hurt me so badly," you may be saying. "I can't forgive them."

Friend, if you won't let go of the old, God won't do the new, and that is a heavy price to pay.

"Well, I prayed and prayed, but my situation still didn't work out. I just don't understand why," you might be saying.

Truth is, you may never understand why. Just let go of the ashes. Learn to trust God. He has a new beginning for you, but you dare not make the mistake of being trapped in the past, living with a victim mentality.

I know of a man who lost his wife in a tragic auto accident more than ten years ago. She was a beautiful, outgoing woman. Now, it's normal to go through a period of grieving. That's the way God made us. If you've lost a job, a marriage, or most certainly a loved one, I'm not saying that you should never feel discouragement or sorrow. But this man was still grieving ten years later! He allowed a season of mourning to turn into a lifetime of mourning.

I tried to encourage him, reminding him that there are good days ahead. But he would never receive that. He was trapped in the past. He was constantly making excuses, blaming God, blaming other people. He'd tell me, "Joel, you just don't know what I've been through. It's just too hard. It's so unfair. I don't understand it."

Now, I don't mean to sound harsh, but over time, I began to realize that the grieving man didn't really want to get well. He liked wallowing in self-pity. He liked the attention that it got him. He became known as "the man who lost his wife." Sadly, he let his tragedy become his identity. To this day he is living a depressed and defeated life.

He's holding on to the ashes. God wants to give him a new beginning, but because he won't let go of the old, he is interfering with God's plan to do something fresh and new in his life.

When you are tempted to sit around feeling sorry for yourself, complaining about how unfair life is, ask yourself a tough question: "Do I really want to get well, or have I gotten comfortable with where I am in life?" Don't ever let your setback become your identity. To put it bluntly, if you were mistreated as you were growing up, you've got to get over that. Quit talking about it. Quit opening up that old wound time and time again. You may have been severely wounded by a divorce; it's time to let it go. Move on. Quit mourning about something that you can't change. Maybe your business partner cheated you out of some money, or you missed out on a big promotion at work. Okay, quit dwelling on it; refrain from talking about it; stop bringing it up to your friends all the time.

God wants to bring beauty in exchange for those ashes. We need to avoid dwelling on anything that reminds us of the pains of the past. Get rid of anything that evokes a negative, hurtful memory. The man I mentioned previously had several newspaper articles about that accident lying on his coffee table at home. Every time he walked by there, he was reminded of the pains of the past. I told him, "Get rid of those things. Put some happy pictures of your wife up. Put some things up that bring back good memories, not all this junk. If you want a new start, you've got to get rid of anything that reminds you of the old."

> Don't ever let your setback become your identity.

In my case, I have never gone back to my father's grave site. I don't want to bring up those memories of my dad. I have good memories of my dad. We have pictures in our house of Daddy with my children, things that bring back happy memories. Certainly, if going to a loved one's grave site brings you peace, fine. But on the other hand, if you're still mourning over what you've lost, thinking about how badly you miss that person, and it's opening up all those old wounds, you are only hurting yourself. That's not healthy. If it's not doing anything positive in your life, don't do it.

Friend, God always has a new beginning. The real question is: Are you willing to move on with your life with a good attitude, knowing that God has a bright future in store?

✎ Today's Prayer for Your Best Life Now ✎

Yes, Father, I want to leave the past in the past and move into the faith-filled future that You have for me. Thank You for the good memories I have, and thank You that the best days are still ahead!

PART FIVE

FINDING STRENGTH
THROUGH ADVERSITY

IT'S NOT ALWAYS EASY

The steps of a good man are ordered by the LORD: and he delighteth in his way.

PSALM 37:23 KJV

LIVING YOUR BEST life now is not always easy; sometimes it is downright difficult. For instance, you may be experiencing some sort of adversity in your life today; you may not be exactly where you want to be physically, emotionally, intellectually, or spiritually. Someone close to you may be hard to get along with. Or maybe you have other obstacles in your path. Regardless of what's going on in your life, don't use that as an excuse to live in discouragement and despair.

Understand, the tough times of life cause us to grow; that's when our faith is stretched. That's when God is doing a work in us. It may be uncomfortable. We may not like it, but if we can keep the right attitude, God has promised to use that difficulty for our good. He'll use it for our advantage.

If God were to remove that adversity, you wouldn't be prepared for what He has in store for you. I know that can be hard to understand. We think, *God, why am I still in this situation? God, why do I have to work around these people I don't like?* Or, *Why am I still having these difficulties?*

That's the wrong approach. Our attitude should be, "God, I

know You're in complete control of my life, and You've got me exactly where You want me to be, so I'm going to stay filled with faith. I'm going to stay full of joy and keep pressing forward, knowing that You will use these difficulties to my advantage."

If God is directing our steps, we can be confident that He is aware of our circumstances.

Your faith is similar to a muscle. It grows stronger through resistance. It is exercised when it's being stretched, when it's being pushed. That's why God does not usually deliver us from adversity overnight. He doesn't remove us from every uncomfortable situation in a split second. He uses those times to build our "spiritual muscles."

Some people live in despair and disappointment, all because their circumstances are not exactly what they desire them to be. People like that are not going to be happy unless everything is going their way, everybody is treating them right, and they are immune from experiencing discomfort. In other words, they probably never will be happy! Besides, that's a very shallow way to live.

If you lose your joy every time something negative happens to you, then the enemy will continue to attack. He'll make sure you always have somebody in your life who irritates you, or some situation that's going to keep you sour. But don't make that mistake.

Our Scripture today says that "the steps of a good man are ordered by the LORD" (Psalm 37:23 KJV). If God is directing our steps, we can be confident that He is aware of our circumstances.

"Well, that can't be right," you may be saying. "After all, I'm uncomfortable; I'm having a problem. Nothing's going my way. That's why I'm so down and discouraged."

No, if you don't learn to be happy where you are, you will never get to where you want to be. You may be dealing with difficult circumstances and may have a thousand reasons why you could be unhappy, but don't slip into that trap.

Choose to enjoy each day in spite of your circumstances. Every day you live with a negative attitude, dominated by your discouragements, is a day you've wasted. And what a shame to waste what God has given us! Understand, adversities are simply a test of your faith. Perhaps God wants to see how you will treat other people when you are not being treated well. He may want to see how you are going to respond if you don't get the promotion you were hoping for. What kind of attitude are you going to have if your prayers aren't answered as quickly as you would like? In the tough times, our characters develop. Something happens on the inside; God is causing us to grow up. If He delivered us instantaneously from every problem, we'd never need any faith. Moreover, we would never develop into the persons He really wants us to be.

The Scripture says, "God causes all things to work together for good to those who love God, to those who are called according to His purpose" (Romans 8:28 NASB). You may be in a difficult situation today. You may be in a hard place in your marriage or on the job; maybe you are in a hard place in your finances.

Friend, God will not allow a difficulty to come into your life unless He has a purpose for it. Granted, there are times when we can't understand what we're going through or why, but we must learn to trust God and believe that He's going to bring some kind of good out of it.

❧ Today's Prayer for Your Best Life Now ❧

God, I may not understand this, but I know You have me here for a reason. This situation may not be good, but I know You will work it for my good. It's stretching me. I know I'm growing, and I'm going to come out of this stronger, happier, healthier, and better off than I was previously.

GOD'S REFINING FIRE

SCRIPTURE READING FOR YOUR BEST LIFE NOW   1 Peter 4:12–5:10

Beloved, do not be surprised at the fiery ordeal among you, which comes upon you for your testing, as though some strange thing were happening to you.

                                   1 PETER 4:12 NASB

WHEN ADVERSITY COMES knocking on the door or calamities occur, some people immediately think they have done something wrong, that God surely must be punishing them. They don't understand that God has a divine purpose for every challenge that comes into our lives. He doesn't send the problems, but sometimes He allows us to go through them.

The Scripture says, "Don't be amazed at the fiery ordeal that's taking place to test your quality, as though something strange were happening" (see 1 Peter 4:12). Notice, the trial is intended to test your character, to test your faith. In other words, "Don't think it's a big deal when you go through these tough times." If you will learn to cooperate with God and be quick to change and correct the areas He brings to light, then you'll pass that test and you will be promoted to a new level.

I've discovered that God is more interested in changing me than He is in changing my circumstances. I'm not saying that God won't deliver us from our struggles by changing the circumstances.

Certainly, He can and often does. But most of the time, we are tested in the areas where we are the weakest.

God often uses adversities to bring to light impurities in our characters, or areas in which we need to improve. God deliberately uses some situations as a mirror, so we can recognize the problem in ourselves and learn to deal with it. He's working something out of us so we can rise to a new level and be the people He really wants us to be.

God may use people and situations in your life to help you better see yourself. Your own husband or wife, your in-laws, or your own children may be the unwitting mirrors that God uses to reveal areas where you need to change.

"Joel, I can't stand my boss. He irritates me to no end. I don't know why I have to work with him day in and day out. When is God ever going to change that man?"

Have you considered that God may want to change *you*? God may have purposely arranged for you to be in close proximity to that person who grates against you. He may be trying to teach you how to love your enemies. Or, He may be trying to toughen you up a little and teach you to have some endurance, to not run from everything that is hard, uncomfortable, or inconvenient.

God deliberately uses some situations as a mirror, so we can recognize the problem in ourselves and learn to deal with it.

God is not going to change anyone you are dealing with until He first changes you. But if you'll quit complaining about everybody around you and, instead, start taking a good look inside and working with God to change you, God will change those other people. Begin today to examine your own heart and see if there are attitudes and motives that you need to change.

220 DAILY READINGS FROM YOUR BEST LIFE NOW

Today's Prayer for Your Best Life Now

Father, I want to be quick to change when You show me areas in which I need to improve. Please give me the courage, strength, and will to make the changes, and the patience to allow Your transforming process to do the complete work in me.

LET GOD CHANGE YOU

*Be truly glad! . . . These trials are only to test your faith,
to see whether or not it is strong and pure . . . So if your
faith remains strong after being tried in the test tube of
fiery trials, it will bring you much praise and glory and
honor on the day of his return.*

1 Peter 1:6–7 TLB

Perhaps you are in a trial today, and you are praying for God to deliver you out of that adverse situation. That is a legitimate prayer, but maybe you're missing the point of why you are being allowed to go through that trying time in the first place. Recognize that God is molding you and refining you.

God often allows you to go through difficult situations to draw out those impurities in your character. You can pray, you can resist, you can bind, you can loose, you can sing and shout, you can do it all, but it's not going to do any good. God is more interested in changing you than He is in changing the circumstances. And the sooner you learn to cooperate with God, the sooner you'll get out of that mess. The quicker you learn your lesson and start dealing with those bad attitudes and start ruling over your emotions, the quicker you'll go to the next level in your spiritual journey. We must recognize the refining purpose of trials. We can't run from everything that's hard in our lives.

Perhaps you get worried and fearful when important things don't go your way. Have you ever thought that God may be allowing those events to teach you to trust Him and to see if you will stay peaceful and calm in the midst of the storm? Have you considered that God may be allowing some of that to teach you how to rule over your emotions? He may be trying to toughen you up, to help you develop some backbone and stability in your life.

Work with Him in the refining process rather than fighting against Him.

We often pray, "God, if You will change my circumstances, then I'll change." No, it works the other way around. We have to be willing to change our attitudes and deal with the issues God brings up; then God will change those circumstances.

God will often permit pressure to be applied in your life to test you, and only as you pass those tests will you advance. He will put people and circumstances in your path that grate on you like sandpaper, but He will use them to rub off your rough edges. You may not always like it; you may want to run from it; you may even resist it, but God is going to keep bringing up the issue again and again, until you pass the test.

Remember, the Bible says, "We are [God's] workmanship" (Ephesians 2:10 NKJV). That means we are a work in progress, not a finished product. Be willing to deal with any issues that God brings up. Work with Him in the refining process rather than fighting against Him.

Scripture says that God is the potter and we are the clay. Clay works best when it is pliable, malleable, and moldable. But if you are hard, crusty, and set in your ways, God will have to pound away on that old, hard clay to get out the lumps.

Certainly, none of us enjoy going through struggles, but you have to understand that your struggle may be an opportunity for advancement and promotion. The very thing you are fighting against so tenaciously may be the springboard that catapults you to a new level of excellence. Your challenges may become your greatest assets.

Without the resistance of air, an eagle can't soar. Without the resistance of water, a ship can't float. Without the resistance of gravity, you and I can't even walk. Without opposition or resistance, there is no potential for progress.

Yet our human tendency is to want everything easily. "God, can't You teach me patience without having to go through the traffic jam? God, can't You teach me how to love and trust You without ever having a problem?"

Unfortunately, there are no shortcuts; there's no easy way to mature physically, emotionally, or spiritually. You must remain determined and work with God. The Bible says, "Work out your own salvation" (Philippians 2:12 NKJV). Salvation is more than a onetime prayer. It is constantly cooperating with God, dealing with the issues He brings up, keeping a good attitude, and allowing Him to change you as He sees fit.

❧ Today's Prayer for Your Best Life Now ❧

Father, I realize that You never promised I would not have trials and adversities. But I also recognize that nothing can touch my life without going through You first, so I will dare to praise You in the midst of my trials. I know You will bring me out stronger and better prepared for the good things You have for me.

FIND A REASON TO GIVE GOD THANKS

Scripture Reading for Your Best Life Now   Luke 17:11–19

It is good to give thanks to the LORD and to sing praises to Your name, O Most High; to declare Your lovingkindness in the morning, and Your faithfulness by night.

PSALM 92:1 NASB

Have you ever considered that perhaps you are not getting your prayers answered because you are not grateful for what God has already done for you? Think of it as a parent. If your child is grateful and he or she sincerely thanks you for what you have done, you want to do more for him or her. On the other hand, if your child is not grateful, and all he or she does is hound you for more, you're not apt to help that child very much.

It's similar with God. The Scripture teaches us that we should continually give God thanks; we should live with an attitude of gratitude.

You may say, "I've been through so many disappointments. I lost my business last year. My marriage didn't work out. I've lost so much. How do you expect me to be grateful?"

But if it had not been for the goodness of God, you could have lost it all. If not for God's mercy, you might not even be here today. Quit looking at what you have lost and start thanking God for what you have left.

My friend Freddie Lamb had a flat tire out on the freeway. As he was on the side of the road changing the tire, a drunk driver smashed his car into him. As a result of the incident, Freddie lost both of his legs beneath the knees.

Several days after the accident, my parents went to the hospital to visit Freddie, thinking that he would be distraught and upset over his loss. But not Freddie. He had a smile on his face and was full of joy. All he could talk about was how God had spared his life. In spite of the tragedy, he still had a grateful attitude. He rose off the bed and said, "Look, Pastor, what's left of my legs can still give God praise."

Freddie wasn't focused on what he didn't have. He was thanking God for what he did have. He may have lost a lot, but he knew if it were not for the goodness of God, he could have lost it all. Today, Freddie Lamb has new artificial limbs, and everywhere he goes, he tells people what God has done for him.

Make a decision today that you're going to be like Freddie. No matter what comes against you, you're going to have a grateful attitude. You're going to find some reason to give God thanks.

Recently, I received a letter from an eighty-seven-year-old lady named Dorothy. She writes down the jokes I tell at the beginning of my sermons, and then she goes to the nursing home to tell them to her friends, to cheer up those she calls the "old people." Interestingly, Dorothy told me, "Joel, nobody at the nursing home knows it, but I have a terminal lung condition. It causes me to cough more than two hundred times a day. But I feel so blessed that I can go up there and make a difference."

No matter what comes against you, have a grateful attitude.

Dorothy epitomizes the attitude God wants us to have when faced with adversity. She's not focused on what's wrong. She's focused on what's right. She could be at home blaming God, and feeling sorry for herself. But no, she's learned the principle that in everything we are to give God thanks.

Perhaps you've lost your joy. You've lost your enthusiasm. You've lost your victory. You would get it back if you would start being more grateful. I heard about a man who was a very negative person. He constantly focused on what he had lost. One day, somebody told him to write down ten things he could be grateful for. He did that, and every morning he went over the list several times. Little by little, his attitude began to change. He got his joy back. He got his victory back. Today he's a totally different person.

When you're tempted to become discouraged, recognize that the root cause can often be traced to having an ungrateful attitude. No matter what comes against you, if you'll do as Freddie and Dorothy did, you can overcome in every situation. Granted, you may have suffered some losses, but thank God that you're still here. You're alive. Make a decision that you're going to be a grateful person. Find some reason to give God thanks. If you'll do that, there's no limit to what God will do in your life.

❧ Today's Prayer for Your Best Life Now ❧

Father, please forgive me for complaining about what I don't have and can't do. From this day forward, please help me to be thankful for what I do have. I thank You and praise You for Your kindness toward me.

HAVE A GRATEFUL ATTITUDE

In everything give thanks: for this is God's will for you in Christ Jesus.

1 Thessalonians 5:18 nasb

Many people go around complaining, always looking at what's wrong. They see the negative in every situation, and then they wonder why they're not happy, why they're not enjoying their lives. Really, it's because they have an ungrateful, unthankful attitude. It's a heart issue, and if they don't get to the root cause and start being more grateful, it's never going to change.

But God didn't give us our mouths to complain. You may not have everything you would like today. In fact, you may be dealing with a lot of problems, but complaining is only going to make matters worse. You need to quit looking at what you *don't* have and start thanking God for what you *do* have. Quit taking inventory of everything that's wrong, and start thanking God for what's right.

The reason many people can't seem to get out of their problems is because they are not grateful for what God has already done for them or what He's already given them. "Well," you say, "you should see the car that I'm driving. It's an old beat-up piece of trash. I can't stand driving that thing."

No, some people would love to have your car. Some people

have to get around by taking the bus, riding a bicycle, or walking. You need to change your perspective and start thanking God that at least you have a car as a means of transportation.

Until you have a grateful attitude, you're going to stay right where you are. "Well, Joel, you don't understand my situation. My husband is so lazy. He doesn't like to do anything. I don't even enjoy his company."

Do you know how many people are lonely today? Do you know how many people would love to have someone to eat dinner with tonight? Your spouse may not be perfect, but you need to change your attitude and start thanking God that at least you have somebody with whom you can share your life. Start being grateful for what God has given you. That's the first step to seeing things improve. Your life might take a radical turn for the better if you'd just change your perspective and start being more grateful.

And remember this: No matter how many negative things you have in your life, somebody has it a whole lot worse than you do. Somebody would love to trade places with you.

You may not have the perfect job; you may not care for your boss. But instead of going around complaining about your workplace, start thanking God that at least you have a job. You could be in an unemployment line. You could be out in the street somewhere. Imagine that you got laid off, and for six or seven months, you couldn't find a new job. You didn't have enough money to pay your bills, and the bank was threatening to foreclose your house because you couldn't make the payments. Then your former employer called you up and offered you that same job back. Do you know how thrilled you would be to have your old job?

What made the difference? Your perspective changed.

We need to remind ourselves, "I may not like this job, but what would I do if I didn't have it? I may not like this house I'm living in, but what would I do if I didn't have my home? I may not particularly enjoy the person to whom I'm married, but what would happen if one day that person was gone?" We need to see our circumstances in a different light.

Some parents perpetually complain about their children. "These children are just driving me nuts. They make such a mess. All I do is clean up after them."

Do you realize that some husbands and wives would love to have children like yours? Some people have spent thousands of dollars, and have gone through all kinds of medical procedures, trying to become pregnant and have children.

Every one of us has a reason to give God thanks.

They would give anything to be able to clean up that mess. You should thank God every day for blessing you with those children.

When you drive to work, instead of complaining about the traffic, why not say, "Father, thank You for giving me this job." When it's time to go to church, instead of complaining that it's too far, too long, or too crowded, why not change your perspective and say, "Father, thank You for the privilege of gathering with other believers to worship."

Every one of us has a reason to give God thanks. If you got out of bed this morning, you can thank God that you're alive. Thank God that you're healthy and have strength. There are lots of people at the medical center who would gladly exchange places with you. Have a grateful attitude.

More than a million people die every single week. Think about that. You were better off than a million other people last week. If you have a roof over your head, you are better off than 75 percent of the world's population. If you have fifteen dollars to your name, you are in the top 8 percent of the world's wealthiest people. Fifteen dollars!

We have so much to be grateful for. We should get in the habit of giving God thanks all day long. Let's start by giving Him thanks for this new day.

∞ Today's Prayer for Your Best Life Now ∞

Thank You, Father, for another day. Thank You for giving me a job. Father, thank You for my family, and for our friends and neighbors. Thank You, Father, for giving me such a great life, not just in heaven one of these days, but right here on earth in the here and now.

DON'T TAKE NORMAL FOR GRANTED

I have learned to be content whatever the circumstances.
Philippians 4:11 niv

Contentment starts in your attitude. It's all in how you choose to see things. You can complain about your boss, or you can thank God that you have a job. You can complain about mowing the lawn, or you can thank God that you have a yard. You can complain about the price of gas, or you can thank God that you have an automobile. It's all in how you choose to see it.

Friend, choose to have a grateful attitude. You may be thinking, *My life is so routine. I just get up, go to work, and come home. I do the same thing day after day. I don't have anything exciting happening to be especially thankful for.*

Many times we don't realize how great we have it until something is taken away. I heard about a young couple who had two children. The dad had a good job and they didn't have any problems to speak of. But then one day the dad said he wasn't feeling well. When he went to the doctor, they discovered that he had a very serious illness. This family spent weeks going to various hospitals in different locations for test after test. Now their time was consumed by medical matters. The doctors finally found a way to treat the father, so for the next several months, he had to go to the hospital every other day to receive treatment. It was a long, drawn-out ordeal, and it totally interrupted the family members' lives.

As the lady was telling the story, she said something that really struck me. She said, "We've been through so much; now, how I long for the mundane. How I long to get back to doing what we used to do. How I long to just go home and sit around with my family at night."

Nobody ever says on their deathbed, "If I had to do it again, I'd spend more time at the office."

What she was saying was, "I didn't realize how great we had it when we didn't have any problems, when we were just going to work, just raising our family. What I thought were boring, unexciting days, I would give anything to have those times back now." Later she said, "I'll never again complain about the mundane."

The truth is, much of life is routine. It's easy to think, *I can't be grateful. I can't be happy. I don't have anything exciting going on.*

But if your health was taken away, or your loved one got sick, or you lost your job, it would change your whole perspective. You would long for the mundane. You would long to get back to where you are right now. Why not make a decision to appreciate what you have? Be grateful for what God has done in your life. Choose to enjoy this day.

Don't take everyday, "normal" life for granted. If you are healthy, have a roof over your head, and have a family, you have so much to be thankful for. Don't wait until something is lost or taken away before you really appreciate what you have. Learn to enjoy what God has given you.

Take time for the people you love. Take time for your family. Quit working all the time. When you come to the end of your life, you will never regret having spent time with your family. Nobody ever says on their deathbed, "If I had to do it again, I'd spend more time at the office. I'd just work a little harder." No, they always say, "I wish I'd spent more time with my family. If I had a chance to live my life again, I'd take more vacations. I'd slow down and smell the roses. I wouldn't live so stressed out."

But you say, "Joel, I'm so busy. I don't have enough time to get everything done as it is!"

That's true, but when you come to the end of your life, if you're like most people, you're still going to have things to do. You're still going to have phone calls to return. You're still going to have appointments to make. Your schedule will never slow down on its own. You must make time for what matters most; make it a priority. If you don't schedule time for the people you love, nobody will do it for you.

I talk to a lot of people who have gone through life-threatening diseases or maybe they had an accident where they almost lost their life. Without fail, they all talk about the same thing—how much more they appreciate each day. They realize that every new sunrise is a gift from God.

We need to realize that in a moment, we could be gone. We have no guarantee that we will be here at this time next year. We need to learn to live each day to the fullest, as though it could be our last. I heard somebody say, "If you had only an hour to live, who would you call? What would you say? And what are you waiting for?"

∼ Today's Prayer for Your Best Life Now ∼

Father, please help me to appreciate every day of life that You give me, and to make every day count. Show me Your priorities for my life—the things that matter most to You—and help me to align my priorities with Yours.

THESE ARE THE GOOD OLD DAYS

SCRIPTURE READING FOR YOUR BEST LIFE NOW   Psalm 71:14–24

*Teach us to number our days, that we may present to
You a heart of wisdom.*

PSALM 90:12 NASB

YOU MAY NOT realize it, but we are living in the good old days.
I'm convinced twenty or thirty years from now most of us will
look back and say, "Those were some great times."

A number of years ago, four of us Osteen kids were working on
staff at Lakewood Church in Houston with our parents. In church
nearly every Sunday, as we sat listening to my father speak, I
leaned over and whispered to Victoria, "We've got to really enjoy
this time. We're not always going to be here together as a family."
Sure enough, as time went on, my sister April and her husband,
Gary, moved away; so did my brother Jim and his wife, Tamara.
And, of course, Daddy went to be with the Lord. Victoria and I
made a point to enjoy those days, because we knew we could
never get that time back.

Make sure you're enjoying your family and special people in
your life. They may not always be there.

A young man with whom I used to play basketball was a fine,
strong athlete, but one day he started having a problem with his
eye. He went to the doctor, and after several tests, they diagnosed

him as having cancer in the eye. Since it seemed a high probability that he was going to lose his vision, he was devastated.

In surgery, the doctors discovered that the problem was behind the eye. But much to their surprise, they found that he didn't have cancer. The problem was caused by an extremely unusual fungus that they were able to remove and save his vision.

When the young man woke up from the operation and heard the good news, he said, "This is the greatest day of my life."

Think about it. He hadn't won the lottery or gotten a big promotion at work. He hadn't purchased a new car or a new home. He had simply received the news that he could continue to see.

He told me, "Joel, now every morning when I get up, I look around on purpose. I gaze in appreciation at my children. I go outside and admire the leaves. I take time to pick up an acorn, and I just stare at it." Because he almost lost his vision, seeing has taken on a whole new meaning for him. He appreciates his sight in a much greater way.

Few of us would say that the greatest day of our lives was waking up and being able to see. But oh, how things change when we find out we may lose something as precious as our sight. If you can see and hear, if you are healthy, if you have family and friends, if you've got a job, food, and a place to live, learn to appreciate those things. Don't go around complaining about what's wrong. Change your attitude and thank God for what you do have.

You may be facing some formidable obstacles in your path. But if you look hard enough you can find some reason to be grateful. The Scripture says, "In everything give thanks" (1 Thessalonians 5:18 NASB). Notice, it doesn't say, "*For* everything give thanks." You don't necessarily thank God for your problems; you thank God in spite of your problems, looking for the good in every situation.

Years ago, I was driving home from church in a pouring rainstorm. I lost control of my car and spun out on the freeway. I crashed into the guardrail, and almost got run over by a huge eighteen-wheeler. Amazingly, I came out of that wreck without a scratch, but my car incurred thousands of dollars' worth of damage.

Later that day, a friend called me and said, "Joel, I heard about your accident. I'm sure you're upset about your car."

God already knows your needs.

I said, "No, I'm not upset about my car one bit. I'm just grateful to be alive." I told him, "I may have lost my car, but if it were not for the goodness of God, I could have lost my life."

I've made up my mind I'm always going to find some reason to be grateful, and I'm going to give God thanks. I'm going to let His praise continually be in my mouth.

Even when I pray, most of my praying these days is simply giving God thanks. I believe we should spend more time *thanking* God than we do asking Him for things. Some people give God their "to do" list: "God, give me this. God, fix this. God, change Aunt Susie. God, give me more money. Amen."

The Scripture says, "We enter into God's presence with praise and thanksgiving" (see Psalm 100:4). If you're just giving God your orders, you're not even getting through the front door, much less entering God's presence.

I like to start off my day by thanking God for the basics: "Father, thank You for my health. Thank You for my children. Thank You for my family. Thank You for my home. Father, thank You for all that You've done for me."

Friend, God already knows your needs. He already knows what you're going to say before you say it. There's nothing wrong with asking God for things—the Scripture clearly instructs us to look to Him to meet our needs—but we should spend more time praising Him for His goodness than requesting His goodies. We should spend more time giving God thanks for what He's already done than we do asking Him to do new things.

I've discovered the more I thank God for what I have, the more God gives me what I don't have. Try it and see. You don't have to beg God; He wants to help you.

Begin today to thank God for who He is and all that He has done for you.

⚛ Today's Prayer for Your Best Life Now ⚛

Father, I thank You for supplying all of my needs. Father, You've done it in the past, and I thank You that You're going to do it again.

KEEP UP ON THE INSIDE

SCRIPTURE READING FOR YOUR BEST LIFE NOW   Psalm 145:8–21

The LORD sustains all who fall and raises up all who are bowed down.

PSALM 145:14 NASB

OUR CIRCUMSTANCES IN life may occasionally knock us down or force us to sit down for a while, but we must not stay down. Even when we are down on the outside, we must see ourselves as getting up on the inside.

You may have received a bad report from the doctor. Maybe you lost your largest client at work. Perhaps you just found out that your child is in trouble. You may be facing some other serious setback, and you feel as though life has caved in on top of you, knocking you off your feet and pushing you into the pits.

But the good news is, you don't have to stay down. Even if you can't get up on the outside, get up on the inside! In other words, have that victor's attitude and mentality. Stay in an attitude of faith. Don't allow yourself to lapse into negative thinking, complaining, or blaming God. Say, "Father, I may not understand this, but I know You are still in control. And You said all things would work together for my good. You said You would take this evil and turn it around and use it to my advantage. So Father, I thank You that You are going to bring me through this!" No matter what you face in life, if you know how to get up on the inside, no adversity can keep you down.

The Scripture says, "When you've done everything you know how to do, just keep on standing firm" (see Ephesians 6:13). You may be in a situation today where you have done your best. You've prayed and believed. You've placed your faith firmly on the truth of God's Word. But it just doesn't look like anything good is happening. Now you're tempted to say, "What's the use? It's never going to change."

Don't give up! Keep standing. Keep praying; keep believing; keep hoping in faith. "Don't cast away your confidence," the Bible teaches, "for payday is coming" (see Hebrews 10:35). Friend, God will reward you if you will keep standing up on the inside. You may be in the hospital or lying flat on your back at home. But even if you cannot stand up physically, nothing can keep you from standing up on the inside. That sickness may have you down physically, but you don't have to be down spiritually or emotionally. You can keep on getting up in your heart, mind, and will.

Maybe you work around people who are always putting you down, mistreating you, trying to make you feel badly about yourself. Let that trash talk go in one ear and out the other. They may try to knock you down on the outside, but they can't knock you down on the inside. Don't let those people steal your joy. Don't let that problem or adversity cause you to become discouraged or depressed. Just keep standing up on the inside.

Keep on getting up in your heart, mind, and will.

I talked to a man who had recently lost his job. He had been making a good salary working in a prestigious position, but then suddenly he was let go. When he first told me what had happened, I was certain that he was going to be distraught. But when he came to see me, he had a big smile on his face and said, "Joel, I just lost my job, but I can't wait to see what God has in store for me next!"

He had been knocked down by circumstances outside his control, but he was still standing up on the inside. He had a victor's mentality. His attitude was: *This thing is not going to defeat me. This thing is not going to steal my joy. I know I'm the victor and not the victim. I know when one door closes, God will open up a bigger and a better door.*

Today, you can say, "Even if the enemy hits me with his best shot, his best will never be good enough. He may knock me down, but he cannot knock me out. When it's all said and done, when the smoke clears and the dust settles, I'm still going to be standing strong." The Bible says no man can take your joy. That means no person can make you live with a negative attitude. No circumstance, no adversity can force you to live in despair. No matter what you are going through or how difficult it may seem, you can stay standing up on the inside. It will take courage; it will definitely take determination, but you can do it if you decide to do so.

❧ Today's Prayer for Your Best Life Now ❧

With Your help, Father, I will refuse to stay down for long. I may get knocked down, or I may fall down, but I will get back up and keep trusting You for a great future.

LEARN TO ENCOURAGE YOURSELF

David was greatly distressed because the people spoke of stoning him . . . But David strengthened himself in the LORD his God.   1 SAMUEL 30:6 NASB

To LIVE YOUR best life now, you must act on your will, not simply your emotions. Sometimes that means you have to take steps of faith even when you are hurting, grieving, or still reeling from some attack of the enemy.

Before he became king of Israel, David and his men were out patrolling one day, when some bandits attacked their city, burned down all the homes, stole their possessions, and kidnapped the women and children. When David and his men returned, they were devastated. But instead of just sitting around mourning over what he had lost, the Bible says that David "encouraged and strengthened himself in the Lord his God" (1 Samuel 30:6 AMP). In other words, he got up on the inside. He said to his men, "Get your armor back on. We're going to attack the enemy." And they did just that. As David and his men persevered, God supernaturally helped them to recover everything that had been stolen. But I don't believe any of that would have happened if David had not first gotten up on the inside.

You may be sitting around waiting for God to change your circumstances. *Then* you're going to be happy; *then* you're going to have a good attitude; *then* you're going to give God praise. But God is waiting on you to get up on the inside. When you do your part, He'll begin to change things and work supernaturally in your life.

Are you going through a dark time in your life? Perhaps some-body deceived you, took advantage of you, or mistreated you, and now you are tempted to sit around mourning over what you have lost, thinking about how unfair it was, and how your life will never be the same. You need to change your attitude. You have to get up on the inside. Develop that victor's mentality and watch what God will begin to do.

> Develop that victor's mentality and watch what God will begin to do.

When you face adversity, don't be a crybaby. Don't be a complainer. Don't wallow in self-pity. Instead, have the attitude of a victor.

You may be weary and tired, worn down, and ready to give up. You may be saying, "I'm never going to break this addiction. I've had it for so long. I wouldn't even know how to function without it." Or, "My income is so low, and my debts are so high; I don't see how my financial situation will ever get better." Or, "I've been praying for years, but it doesn't look as though my children want to serve God." "I've had about as much as I can take."

Don't allow yourself to wave the white flag of surrender. You must get out of that defeated mentality and start thinking and be-lieving positively. Your attitude should be: *I'm coming out of this thing! I may have been sick for a long time, but I know this sick-ness didn't come to stay. It came to pass. I may have struggled with this addiction for years, but I know my day of deliverance is coming. My children may not be doing right, but as for me and my house, we will serve the Lord.*

You must show the enemy that you're more determined than he is. Shout aloud if you must, "I'm going to stand in faith even if I have to stand my whole lifetime! I'm going to keep standing up on the inside, no matter how long it takes."

God wants you to be a winner, not a whiner. There is no reason for you to be perpetually living "under the circumstances," always down, always discouraged. No matter how many times you get knocked down, keep getting back up. God sees your resolve. He sees your determination. And when you do everything you can do, that's when God will step in and do what you can't do.

❧ Today's Prayer for Your Best Life Now ❧

Father, I choose to rule my emotions, rather than allowing them to dominate me. Please help me to act on what I know is right and true according to Your Word, rather than on outward appearances, feelings, or discouraging information. With Your help, I will be victorious!

PRISONERS OF HOPE

SCRIPTURE READING FOR YOUR BEST LIFE NOW   Joel 2:12–32

In the world you have tribulation, but take courage; I have overcome the world.

JOHN 16:33 NASB

ADVERSITIES AND HARDSHIPS are opportunities for us to go higher. Consequently, God does not prevent every negative thing from coming into your life. In fact, Jesus said, "In this life you will have trouble." "Unfair things will happen to you," He said, but here's the key: "Be of good cheer, for I have overcome the world."

Throughout the Scripture, God says if we'll keep the right attitude, if we'll stay full of joy and full of hope, even though He may not stop all the trouble, when we come out, we won't be the same as we were before. We'll be more blessed, healthy, and prosperous, better off than we were previously.

I think about Joseph. His brothers were so jealous of him, they sold him into slavery. Other young men his age, no doubt, were out having a good time, enjoying their lives. But Joseph was confined, living in a foreign land, having to work all the time. It was unfair; worse yet, Joseph's heartache and pain were caused by somebody else's poor choices and somebody else's bad attitude.

But God saw that injustice. God said in the book of Joel, "I will restore the years that have been stolen from you" (see Joel 2:25). Somehow, some way, God can make up all those years. That's what He did for Joseph. Even though Joseph spent thirteen years in slavery and in prison, God made it all up to him. When he came out, he didn't have to go back home and start all over. No, he came out promoted and increased. He now had a position of honor as the prime minister of all Egypt, second in command only to Pharaoh.

God took the adversity and injustice, and because Joseph kept the right attitude, God brought him out much better than he was before. In other words, God made the enemy pay for bringing the injustice into Joseph's life.

Friend, God is keeping the records in your life, as well. If somebody has mistreated you and done you wrong, don't sit around feeling sorry for yourself. Let hope fill your heart. Know that God will bring you out with twice what you had before. God will never waste anything that you go through.

None of us enjoy tough times. But we can stay filled with hope, knowing that God will never waste the pain. He will always use it to our advantage.

Had Joseph not experienced that adversity, he would not have received the promotion that led to his powerful position. In your times of disappointment and trouble, instead of getting down and discouraged, start believing to come out better off than you were before. Put your faith out there, and remind yourself that God wants to restore good things back to you. You simply need to stay filled with hope, and start expecting things to change.

Remind yourself that God wants to restore good things back to you.

The Bible tells us in Zechariah that we should be "prisoners of hope." So many people go around discouraged and defeated. They live with anger, resentment, and bitterness, rather than hope. "But Joel, you don't know what I've been through. You don't know how bad my marriage has been, or how deeply I'm in debt."

No, quit dwelling on all of that. Don't magnify your problems. Magnify your God. The bigger you make God, the smaller your problems become, and the more faith will rise in your heart.

The Scripture teaches that we shouldn't look at the things that are seen, but at the things that are not seen; for the things that are seen are only temporary, but the things that are seen through our eyes of faith are eternal (see 2 Corinthians 4:18). One translation says, "The things that are seen are subject to change."

That means your health may not look too good today, but that's subject to change. Your finances may look pretty dismal, but they are subject to change. Nothing may be going right in your life, but it's all subject to change. When you look at your child who's not living right, instead of getting discouraged and losing your hope, look at him or her and say, "You are subject to change." You may need to look at your checkbook and say, "This is subject to change." Maybe your boss is not treating you right. He's being rude and disrespectful. Just smile and say, "You are subject to change." (You probably shouldn't say that to his face, or your job may be subject to change!)

If you want to see God restore what's been stolen from you, stay filled with hope. You have to get up each morning expecting things to change, expecting good things to happen. You need to know that in a moment of time, God could turn it all around. Suddenly you could get your miracle. Suddenly God could bring someone new into your life. Suddenly you could get that promotion. All it takes is one "suddenly." In a split second, with one touch of God's favor, everything can change.

Our attitude should be, *I'm going to take back what belongs to me. I'm not going to sit around mourning over what I've lost. I may have been knocked down, but I'm not going to stay down. I'm going to get back up again, knowing that Almighty God is on my side, and if God be for me, who dares be against me?* And if you'll stay filled with hope, God will restore you, and like Joseph, you'll come out twice as strong, twice as healthy, twice as prosperous. God will make the enemy pay double for bringing that adversity into your life.

❦ Today's Prayer for Your Best Life Now ❦

Help me to believe, Father, that my circumstances are "subject to change," not simply because of me, but because You are helping me to overcome that adversity, and You will bring me out even better than before.

BETTER DAYS AHEAD

The LORD restored the fortunes of Job when he prayed for his friends, and the LORD increased all that Job had twofold.

JOB 42:10 NASB

HAVE YOU EVER felt robbed or cheated by life? You may have experienced some unfair situations in which somebody did you wrong or mistreated you. Perhaps you are having problems in a relationship, or in your marriage, or with a child. Or maybe you've struggled financially, and you don't see how you can ever get ahead. Life has been one setback after another. If that sounds like you, I have good news for you: God wants to restore everything that has been stolen from you. He wants to restore your joy, peace, health, finances, and your family. And when God restores, He doesn't leave you as you were before bad things happened to you; He brings you out *better* than you were previously.

For instance, in the Bible, if a thief was caught stealing, he had to repay his victim seven times what he stole. In another place, Scripture commands that the thief repay four times as much. God Himself said through the prophet Isaiah, "I will pay you back double for all the unfair things that have happened" (see Isaiah 61:7).

When you face trouble or somebody does you wrong, instead

of getting discouraged, your attitude should be, "Father, I thank You, that I'm now in position to receive double. I know I'm going to come out stronger, healthier, and happier than I've ever been."

God does not want to bring you out of your adversities all beaten up and bedraggled; no, you are not simply a survivor, you are "more than a conqueror" (see Romans 8:37). He wants to bring you out promoted and increased, with abundance. Beyond that, God wants to make the enemy pay for the wrongs done to you, His child.

If you're in a tough situation today, you need to develop a restoration mentality. Mentally encourage yourself that God is going to turn your situation around. Remind yourself that you are a victor and not a victim. You don't just defeat the enemy, you gather up all the spoils. You come out better than before, blessed to overflowing.

In the Scripture we read of Job, a good man who loved God and had a heart to do what's right. Yet in a few weeks' time, he lost his business, his flocks and herds, his family, and his health. Things could not get any worse for Job, and I'm sure he was tempted to be bitter. He could have said, "God, it's not fair. I don't understand why this is happening to me."

His own wife told him, "Job, just curse God and die."

But no, Job knew that God is a God of restoration. He knew God could turn any situation around. And his attitude was, *Even if I die I'm going to die trusting God. I'm going to die believing for the best.*

Develop a restoration mentality.

When it was all said and done, God not only turned Job's calamity around, He brought Job out with twice what he had before. He had twice as many cattle, twice as many sheep. He got his health back, and God gave him a new family. God restored double what the enemy had stolen. Amazingly, the Scripture says, "The latter part of Job's life was more blessed than the first part" (see Job 42:12).

Maybe you need to be reminded today that God wants the rest of your life to be more blessed than the first part. Despite what you've been through, or how somebody has treated you, no matter what the medical report says, or what your bank statement says, God is saying, "I want to make the rest of your life happier and more fulfilled than you can even imagine." God wants to bring you out to a flourishing finish. In other words, God is saying the best is yet to come.

⋙ Today's Prayer for Your Best Life Now ⋘

Father, I dare to believe that You are going to turn around those conditions in my life over which I have no control, situations in which someone has chosen to do evil against me. I know You reward those who trust You, so I will continue to believe that You are going to restore all that has been stolen from me.

PART SIX

LIVE TO GIVE

GOD IS A GIVER

God so loved the world, that he gave his only begotten Son.

JOHN 3:16 KJV

"W HAT'S IN IT for me?" everyone wants to know nowadays. Many people are blatantly and unashamedly living for themselves. They're not interested in other people. They won't take time to help others in need. They focus only on what they want, what they need, what they feel will most benefit themselves. Ironically, this selfish attitude condemns them to living shallow, unrewarding lives. No matter how much they acquire for themselves, they are never satisfied.

God, however, is a giver, and if you want to experience a new level of God's joy, if you want Him to pour out His blessings and favor in your life, then you must learn to be a giver and not a taker. Quit trying to figure out what everybody can do for you, and start trying to figure out what you can do for somebody else. We were not made to function as self-involved people, thinking only of ourselves. No, God created us to be givers. And you will never be truly fulfilled as a human being until you learn the simple secret of how to give your life away.

You may not realize it, but it is extremely selfish to be dwelling on your problems, always thinking about what you want or need, and hardly noticing the many needs of others all around you. One of the best things you can do if you're having a problem is to help solve somebody else's problem. If you want your dreams to come to pass, help someone else fulfill his or her dreams. Start sowing some seeds so God can bring you a harvest. When we meet other people's needs, God always meets our needs.

> When we meet other people's needs, God always meets our needs.

We were created to give, not simply to please ourselves. If you miss that truth, you will miss the abundant, overflowing, joy-filled life that God has in store for you. But when you reach out to other people in need, God will make sure that your own needs are supplied. If you're lonely or down and discouraged today, don't sit around feeling sorry for yourself. Get your mind off yourself and go help meet someone else's need. Go visit the nursing home or a children's hospital. Call a friend and encourage that person. If you're struggling financially, go out and help somebody who has less than you have. You need to sow some seeds so God can bring you a harvest.

You may say, "Joel, I don't have anything to give." Sure you do! You can give a smile. You can give a hug. You can do some menial but meaningful task for someone. For example, you could mow somebody's lawn. You could go to the grocery store or make a meal for a person who is shut in and unable to get to the store. You can visit someone in the hospital or in a senior citizens' center. You can write somebody an encouraging letter. Somebody needs what you have to share. Somebody needs your smile. Somebody needs your love. Somebody needs your friendship. Somebody needs your encouragement. God didn't make us to function as "Lone Rangers." He created us to be free, but He did not intend for us to be independent of each other. We really do need one another. If you want God to bless your life, start being a blessing to others.

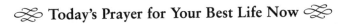 **Today's Prayer for Your Best Life Now**

Father, please help me to get my eyes off myself and to see the many needs in people all around me. May I be a means of help, comfort, and encouragement to someone else today.

GOD WILL TAKE CARE OF YOU

Scripture Reading for Your Best Life Now   Luke 7:27–49

One man gives freely, yet gains even more; another withholds unduly, but comes to poverty.

PROVERBS 11:24 NIV

WHEN YOU CENTER your life around yourself, not only do you miss out on God's best, but you rob other people of the joy and blessings that God wants to give them through you. The Scripture says, "We should encourage one another daily" (see Hebrews 3:13). It's easy to criticize and condemn, to point out everyone's flaws and failures. But God wants us to build people up, to be a blessing, speaking words of faith and victory into their lives.

It doesn't cost anything or take a lot of time to give somebody a compliment. What does it cost to tell your wife, "I love you. You're great. I'm glad you're mine"? How long does it take to tell your employee, "You are doing a fine job. I appreciate your hard work"?

Many people think those nice thoughts, but fail to verbalize them. It's not enough to *think* kind compliments; we need to express them. As the old saying puts it: "Love is not love until you give it away." We should get up each morning with an attitude that says: *I'm going to make somebody else happy today. I'm going to help meet somebody else's need.* Don't go through life as a taker; become a giver.

"But Joel, I have so many problems and so many needs of my own . . ."

Yes, but if you get your mind off your problems and begin to help others, you won't have to worry about your needs. God will take care of them for you. Something supernatural happens when we get our eyes off ourselves and turn to the needs of those around us.

The Old Testament teaches, "When you feed the hungry, when you clothe the naked, when you encourage the oppressed, then your life is going to break forth like the dawn. Then your healing is going to quickly come" (see Isaiah 58:7–8). In other words, when you reach out to hurting people, that's when God ensures that your needs are supplied. When you focus on being a blessing, God makes sure that you are always blessed in abundance.

When my mother was diagnosed with terminal cancer back in 1981, she could easily have come home and just sunk into a deep pit of depression. But Mother didn't do that. She didn't stay focused on herself, and she refused to dwell on that sickness. In her time of greatest need, she went to church and prayed for other people who were sick and in need. She sowed those seeds of healing. And just as the Scripture says, as she began to help other people in need, her light broke forth like the dawn, and her own healing came.

> God makes sure that you are always blessed in abundance.

I'm convinced that many people would receive the miracle they have been praying about if they would simply turn their attention away from their own needs and problems, and start to focus on being a blessing to other people. All too often we spend most of our time trying to be blessed. "God, what can You do for me? God, here's my prayer list. Can I have it by next Tuesday?"

We need to look for opportunities to share God's love, His gifts, and His goodness with others. The truth is, the more you help others, the more God will make sure that you are helped.

You can do this in many practical ways. If you have things lying around your house or in storage that you are never going to use again, why not give those things away to someone who could use them? Those extra things aren't doing you any good stacked in your attic, basement, or garage. If it's not meeting a need, turn it into a seed!

Our minds can conjure up all kinds of excuses when God begins unclasping our sticky fingers. Human nature wants to hold on to everything. But you probably have some clothes you haven't worn in years; cooking utensils still packed in boxes from your last move, books, your children's crib and baby clothing, and all sorts of other things that you haven't used in ages! Most clutter experts say, "If you haven't used an item within the past year, give it away!" If it's not meeting a need, turn it into a seed. Remember, we will reap what we sow. When you do good for other people, that's when God is going to make sure that His abundant blessings overtake you.

If you want to live your best life now, you must develop a lifestyle of giving: living to give instead of living to get. Have an attitude that says, *Who can I bless today?* rather than *How can I be blessed today?*

✖ Today's Prayer for Your Best Life Now ✖

Father, I know You have blessed me, and I want to be a blessing to others. Help me to not be simply a consumer of Your blessings, but a person who passes blessings on to others.

BLESSED TO BE A BLESSING

SCRIPTURE READING FOR YOUR BEST LIFE NOW   Genesis 12:1–4;
13:14–17; 15:1

*Remember the words of the Lord Jesus, how he said, It
is more blessed to give than to receive.*

ACTS 20:35 KJV

GOD WILL NOT fill a closed fist with good things. God is a giver,
and you are never more like God than when you give.

God promised the Old Testament patriarch Abraham, "I will
bless you [with abundant increase of favors] and make your name
famous and distinguished, and you will be a blessing" (Genesis
12:2 AMP). We often read such promises, and say, "All right, God!
Come on; pour out Your blessings on me!" But notice, there's a
catch. We must do something; better yet, we must *be* something.
God is implying that we will not be blessed simply so we can live
lavishly or self-indulgently. We will be blessed *to be* a blessing. Indeed, unless we are willing to be a blessing, God will not pour out
His favor and goodness in our lives. We will receive from God in
the same measure we give to others.

"But Joel, you just don't understand. I don't have anything
extra to give."

Perhaps not. But it all depends on your attitude. You must be
faithful in the little you have right now before God will bless you
with more. A lot of people say, "God, when are You going to bless

me?" But if we'd listen more carefully, maybe we'd hear God saying, "When are you going to start *being* a blessing?"

Giving is a spiritual principle. Whatever you give will be given back to you. If you give a smile, you will receive smiles from others. If you are generous to people in their time of need, God will make sure that other people are generous to you in your time of need. Interesting, isn't it? What you make happen for others, God will make happen for you.

Nothing pleases God any more than when we take care of one of His children.

The Bible says, "When you help the poor you are lending to the Lord" (Proverbs 19:17 TLB). You may be thinking, *Well, if I had more money, I would give more.*

No, that's where you miss it. You have to start right where you are. You must be faithful with what you have, then God will trust you with more. You may not have a lot of extra money to give, but you can buy somebody's dinner every once in a while. You can give somebody a kind word. You can go out of your way to pray for somebody in need.

Now is the time to develop an attitude of giving. Friend, the closest thing to the heart of our God is helping hurting people. God loves when we sing and when we pray. He loves when we come together to celebrate His goodness. But nothing pleases God any more than when we take care of one of His children. Jesus said, "If you even give as much as a cup of water to somebody in need, I see it and I'm going to reward you" (see Matthew 10:42). He said, "Inasmuch as you did it to one of the least of these My brethren, you did it to Me" (Matthew 25:40 NKJV).

Somebody needs what you have to give. It may not be your money; it may be your time. It may be your listening ear. It may be your arms to encourage. It may be your smile to uplift. Who knows? Maybe just putting your arm around somebody and letting him or her know that you care can help begin to heal that person's heart. Maybe you can give a rescuing hug.

John Bunyan, author of the classic book *The Pilgrim's Progress*, said, "You have not lived today until you have done something for someone who cannot pay you back." Make a decision that today you will be on the lookout for somebody you can bless.

✑ Today's Prayer for Your Best Life Now ✑

Father, I know that You are a giver, and I want to be like You. Please help me to hold loosely those things You have placed in my hands, and help me to always be ready to give to others in the same way You have given to me.

KINDNESS PAYS OFF

SCRIPTURE READING FOR YOUR BEST LIFE NOW   Matthew 5:38–48

Be kind to one another, tender-hearted, forgiving each
other, just as God in Christ also has forgiven you.
EPHESIANS 4:32 NASB

How YOU TREAT other people has a great impact on the degree
of blessings and favor of God you will experience in your life. Are
you good to people? Are you kind and considerate? Do you speak
and act with love in your heart and regard other people as valuable and special? Friend, you can't treat people poorly and expect
to be blessed. You can't be rude and inconsiderate and expect to
live in victory.

The Bible says, "See that none of you repays another with evil
for evil, but always aim to show kindness and seek to do good to
one another and to everybody" (1 Thessalonians 5:15 AMP). Notice the words *aim* and *seek* in this verse. God is saying we must
be proactive. We should be on the lookout to share His mercy,
kindness, and goodness with people. Moreover, we need to be
kind and do good to people even when they don't deserve it. We
need to walk in love and be courteous even when somebody is un-
kind to us.

When that coworker walks by you and doesn't give you the
time of day, God expects you to go the extra mile and be friendly
to him anyway. If you are on the phone and somebody speaks

harshly or is discourteous to you, it's easy to think, *I'll just tell her off and then hang up. She doesn't know me. She's never going to see me.* But God expects us to be kinder and more considerate than that.

When that employee at the grocery store checkout counter is curt with you, your initial response may be to act rudely in return. That's the easy way; anybody can do that. But God wants us to live by higher standards. The Bible says, "We are to love our enemies. We are to do good to them that spitefully use us" (see Luke 6:27–31).

If somebody flies off the handle at you, instead of retaliating and giving them a piece of your mind, why not show them some of God's grace and mercy? Aim for kindness and give them a word of encouragement. After all, you don't know what they may be going through. That person's child may be in the hospital. His or her mate may have just walked out; they may be living in hell on earth. If you return their venom with more vitriol, you could escalate the conflict, or your response could be the final straw that causes them to give up and sink into utter despair. Neither scenario is pleasing to God.

When somebody doesn't treat you right, you have a golden opportunity to help heal a wounded heart. Keep in mind, hurting people often hurt other people as a result of their own pain. If somebody is inconsiderate, you can almost be certain that they have some unresolved issues inside. They have some major problem, anger, resentment, or heartache they are trying to cope with or overcome. The last thing they need is for you to make matters worse by responding angrily.

Hurting people often hurt other people as a result of their own pain.

Evil is never overcome by more evil. If you mistreat people who are mistreating you, you will make matters worse. When you express anger to somebody who has been angry with you, it's like adding fuel to a fire. No, we overcome evil with good. When somebody hurts you, the only way you can overcome it is by showing them mercy, forgiving them, and doing what is right.

Today, take the high road and be kind and courteous to everyone you meet. God will see what you're doing, and He will make sure your good actions and attitude will overcome that evil. If you'll keep doing the right thing, you will come out far ahead of where you would have been had you fought fire with fire.

The Bible teaches us that God is our vindicator. He will not let you lose out. You may think you're getting the short end of the stick, but when it's all said and done, God will make sure that you don't lose anything truly valuable. Moreover, He'll make sure you get your just reward. Your responsibility is to remain calm and peaceable even when those around you are not.

≫ Today's Prayer for Your Best Life Now ≫

With Your love in me, Father, I know I can express kindness even to someone who is not kind to me. Help me to respond lovingly and with compassion to those people who may be having a bad day and are in need of some encouragement.

GOD INTENDS IT FOR GOOD

As for you, you meant evil against me, but God meant it for good in order to bring about this present result, to preserve many people alive.

GENESIS 50:20 NASB

IF SOMEBODY IS not treating you right today, go out of your way to be kinder than usual to that person. If your husband is not serving God, don't go around beating him over the head with your Bible, preaching at him, nagging him, coercing him to attend church with you. No, just start being extra kind to him. Start loving him in a fresh way. The Bible teaches, "It is the goodness of God that leads people to repentance" (see Romans 2:4). God's goodness expressed through you will overcome evil. Friend, love never fails.

If anybody had a right to return evil instead of love, it was Joseph, the young man with the distinctive coat of many colors. His brothers hated him so much, they threw him into a deep pit and were going to kill him, but "out of the kindness of their hearts" they decided instead to sell him into slavery. Years went by, and Joseph experienced all sorts of troubles and heartaches. But Joseph kept a good attitude, and God continued to bless him. After thirteen years of being in prison for a crime he didn't commit, God supernaturally promoted him to the second-highest position in Egypt.

Joseph was in charge of the food supply when a famine struck the land, and his brothers traveled to Egypt, hoping to buy provisions for their families. At first they didn't recognize their long-lost brother. Joseph finally said, "Don't you know who I am? I am Joseph, your brother. I'm the one you threw into the pit. I'm the one you tried to kill, the brother you sold into slavery."

> If you will choose to let go, you can overcome with good.

Can you imagine what was going through his brothers' minds? Imagine the fear that must have gripped their hearts! This was Joseph's opportunity to pay back his brothers for the years of pain and suffering they had caused him. Now their lives were in his hands.

Joseph could have ordered them killed or imprisoned for life. But Joseph said, "Don't be afraid. I'm not going to harm you. I'm going to do good to you. I'm going to give you all the food you need."

No wonder God's hand of favor was on Joseph in such a strong way. Joseph knew how to extend mercy. Joseph knew how to treat people right.

The Bible says, "Love doesn't hold a grudge. Love doesn't harbor unforgiveness" (see 1 Corinthians 13:5). You may have people in your life who have done you great wrong, and you have a right to be angry and bitter. You may feel as though your whole life has been stolen away by somebody who has mistreated you or deceived you. But if you will choose to let go of your grudge and forgive them, you can overcome that evil with good. You can get to the point where you can look at the people who have hurt you and return good for evil. If you do that, God will pour out His favor in your life in a fresh way. He will honor you; He will reward you, and He'll make those wrongs right.

When you can bless your worst enemies and do good to those who have used or abused you, that's when God will take that evil and turn it around for good. No matter what you've gone through, no matter who hurt you or whose fault it was, let it go. Don't try to get even. Don't hold a grudge. Don't try to pay them back. God says show mercy. Aim for kindness. Seek to do good.

You may be thinking, *But Joel, that's just not fair!*

No, it's not. But life is not fair. We have to remember that God is the One keeping the score. He is in control. And when you bless your enemies, you will never lose. God will always make it up to you.

❧ Today's Prayer for Your Best Life Now ❧

I dare to believe, Father, that You can take even the bad things that happen to me and transform them into something good and useful, not merely in my own life, but in the lives of others around me.

WHEN SOMEONE TAKES
ADVANTAGE OF YOU

SCRIPTURE READING FOR YOUR BEST LIFE NOW   Genesis 13:1–18

*Abraham never wavered in believing God's promise. In
fact, his faith grew stronger, and in this he brought glory
to God.*

ROMANS 4:20 NLT

WHEN YOU BLESS someone else, you never lose out. Even if
someone takes advantage of your good nature, God will not allow
your generosity to go unrewarded. For instance, when God told
Abraham to pack up his family and head toward a better land,
Abraham moved all his flocks, his herds, his family, and even his
extended family members. They traveled for months and finally
made it to their new land. After living there for a while, they discovered that the portion of land where they settled wasn't able to
support them with enough food and water for all the people and
their flocks and herds.

Abraham said to his nephew Lot, "We need to split up." He
said, "You choose whichever part of the land you would like to
have, and I'll take whatever is left." Notice how kind Abraham
was to his nephew.

Lot looked around and saw a beautiful valley with lush green
pastures and rolling hills and ponds. He said, "Abraham, that's
what I want. That's where my part of the family will settle." Abra-

ham said, "Fine; go and be blessed." Abraham could have said, "Lot, you're not going to have that land. That's the best land. I've done all the work. I've led this journey. God spoke to me, not to you. I should get the first choice." Abraham didn't do that. He believed that God would make it up to him.

But I'm sure when Abraham took one look at the land left over for him, he was disappointed nonetheless. His portion was arid, barren, desolate wasteland. Think of it; Abraham had traveled a long distance. He'd gone to great effort in search of a better life for his family members. Now, because of his generosity and kind heart, he was relegated to living on the scruffy part of the land. I'm sure he thought, *God, why do people always take advantage of my goodness? God, why do I always get the short end of the stick? That boy Lot wouldn't have had anything if I hadn't given it to him.*

Maybe you feel that you're the one who's doing all the giving in some situation. Perhaps you are the parent of an ungrateful child. Maybe your former spouse is taking advantage of you in a divorce settlement. Possibly your company is talking about "downsizing" after you have given them the best years of your life. Perhaps you are the one who's always going the extra mile. You're the peacemaker in the family. Because people know you are kind, generous, and friendly, they tend to take advantage of you or not appreciate you.

But God sees your integrity. Nothing that you do goes unnoticed by God. He's keeping the records, and He will reward you in due time. That's what He did for Abraham.

Nothing that you do goes unnoticed by God.

In essence, God told Abraham, "Because you treated your relative kindly, because you went the extra mile to do what is right, I'm not going to give you a small portion of land; I'm going to give you an abundant blessing. I'm going to give you hundreds and hundreds of acres; miles and miles of land. All that you can see is going to be yours."

Don't grow weary in well-doing. God is a just God, and He sees not just what you are doing but why you are doing it. God judges our motives as well as our actions. And because of your unselfishness, because you prefer others, because you're aiming for kindness, one day God will say to you as He did to Abraham, "As far as you can see, I'm going to give it to you."

Sometimes when we're good to people and we go the extra mile, we have a tendency to think, *I'm letting people walk all over me. I'm letting them take advantage of me. They're taking what rightfully belongs to me.*

That's when you have to say, "Nobody is taking anything from me. I am freely giving it to them. I'm blessing them on purpose, knowing that God is going to make it up to me." Today, look for an opportunity to do something extra to bless someone who doesn't deserve it. God will honor you for your gesture.

∝ Today's Prayer for Your Best Life Now ∝

Thank You, Father, that nobody can take anything away from me that You are not able to restore. I will live unselfishly as a manager of all that You have given me. I will trust You, and rather than clutching what is legitimately mine, I will live with my hands and heart open to others.

HAVE A HEART OF COMPASSION

SCRIPTURE READING FOR YOUR BEST LIFE NOW   Matthew 9:35–38

*Live in harmony with one another; be sympathetic, love
as brothers, be compassionate and humble.*

1 PETER 3:8 NIV

EVERYWHERE YOU LOOK these days, you can see people who are
hurting. Some people are extremely discouraged; many have broken dreams. Others have made mistakes, and now their lives are
in a mess. They need to feel God's compassion and His uncondi-
tional love. They don't need somebody to judge and criticize them,
or to tell them what they're doing wrong. (In most cases, they already know that!) They need somebody to bring hope, somebody
to bring healing, somebody to show God's mercy. Really, they're
looking for a friend, somebody who will be there to encourage
them, who will take the time to listen to their story and genuinely
care.

We're all so busy. We have our own priorities and important
plans and agendas. Often, our attitude is: *I don't want to be inconvenienced. Don't bother me with your problems. I've got
enough problems of my own.* But the Scripture says, "If anyone
sees his brother in need yet closes his heart of compassion, how
can the love of God be in him?" (see 1 John 3:17). Interesting, isn't
it? God's Word implies that we each have a heart of compassion,
but the question is whether it is open or closed.

Furthermore, the Bible says, "We are to continually walk in love, being guided by love and following love" (see 2 John 6). When God puts love and compassion in your heart toward someone, He's offering you an opportunity to make a difference in that person's life. You must learn to follow that love. Don't ignore it. Act on it. Somebody needs what you have to give.

Do you take time to make people feel better about themselves?

God has placed in you the potential to have a kind, caring, gentle, loving spirit. You have the ability to empathize, to feel what other people are feeling. Because you were created in the image of God, you have the moral capacity to experience God's compassion in your heart right now. But too often, because of our own selfishness, we choose to close our hearts to others.

How can you tell if your heart is open or closed? Easy. Are you frequently concerned about other people, or are you concerned about only yourself? Do you take time to make a difference, to encourage others, to lift their spirits, to make people feel better about themselves? Do you follow the flow of love that God puts in your heart toward somebody in need? Or are you too busy with your own plans? If you want to live your best life now, you must make sure that you keep your heart of compassion open. Be on the lookout for people you can bless. Be willing to be interrupted and inconvenienced every once in a while if it means you can help to meet somebody else's need.

If you study the life of Jesus, you will discover that He always took time for people. He was never too busy with His own agenda, with His own plans. He wasn't so caught up in Himself that He was unwilling to stop and help a person in need. He could have easily said, "Listen, I'm busy. I have a schedule to keep. I'm on My way to the next city, and I've already been delayed." But no, Jesus had compassion for people. He was concerned about what they were going through, and He willingly took the time to help. He freely gave of His life. I believe He demands nothing less from those who claim to be His followers today.

Many people are unhappy and are not experiencing life to its fullest because they've closed their hearts to compassion. They are motivated by only what they want and what they think they need. They rarely do anything for anybody else unless they have an ulterior goal in mind. They are self-involved and self-centered.

But if you want to experience God's abundant life, you must get your focus off yourself and start taking time to help other people. Sometimes if we would just take the time to listen to people, we could help initiate a healing process in their lives. So many people today have hurt and pain bottled up inside them. They have nobody they can talk to; they don't really trust anybody anymore. If you can open your heart of compassion and be that person's friend—without judging or condemning—and simply have an ear to listen, you may help lift that heavy burden. You don't have to know all the answers. You just need to care.

We need to learn to be better listeners. Don't always be so quick to give your opinion. Be sensitive to what the real need is in the person you hope to help. Too frequently, what we really want to do is just give them a quick word of encouragement, a semi-appropriate Scripture verse, and a fifteen-second prayer; then we can go on and do what we want to do. Instead, take the time today to hear someone with your heart, to show that person you are concerned, and that you really care.

✑ Today's Prayer for Your Best Life Now ✑

Father, please forgive me for the times I have missed opportunities to show compassion to someone You brought into my life. Help me to be sensitive to Your voice speaking within me, directing me how I can best help someone else.

HOW TO HAVE A BIG HARVEST

SCRIPTURE READING FOR YOUR BEST LIFE NOW   Genesis 26:12–32

A generous man will prosper; he who refreshes others will himself be refreshed.

PROVERBS 11:25 NIV

THE REASON MANY people are not growing is because they are not sowing. They are living self-centered lives. Unless they change their focus and start reaching out to others, they will probably remain in a depressed condition, emotionally, financially, socially, and spiritually.

The Scripture says, "Whatever a man sows, that he will also reap" (Galatians 6:7 NKJV). All through the Bible, we find the principle of sowing and reaping. Just as a farmer must plant some seeds if he hopes to reap the harvest, we, too, must plant some good seeds in the fields of our families, careers, businesses, and personal relationships.

What if the farmer decided that he didn't really feel like planting, that he was tired, so he "felt led" to sit around and hope the harvest would come in? He'd be waiting around his whole life! No, he must get the seed in the ground. That's the principle God established. In the same way, if we want to reap good things, we, too, must sow some good seeds. Notice, we reap what we sow. If you want to reap happiness, you have to sow some "happiness" seeds by making other people happy. If you want to reap financial blessings, you must sow financial seeds in the lives of others. If you want to reap friendships, you should sow a seed and be a friend.

Some people say, "Joel, I've got a lot of problems of my own. I don't care about sowing seeds. I want to know how I can get out of my mess." This *is* how you can get out of your mess. If you want God to solve your problems, help solve somebody else's problem.

In biblical times, a great famine struck the land of Canaan. People didn't have any food or water, and they were in desperate need. So Isaac did something that people without insight may have thought rather odd: "In the middle of that famine, Isaac sowed a seed in the land. And in the same year he received one hundred times what he planted and the Lord rewarded him greatly" (see Genesis 26:12). In his time of need, Isaac didn't wait around, expecting someone else to come to his rescue. No, he acted in faith. He rose up in the midst of that famine and sowed a seed. God supernaturally multiplied that seed, and it brought him out of his need.

Maybe you are in some sort of famine today. It could be a financial famine, or maybe you're simply famished for friends. It's possible you need a physical healing. Perhaps you need peace in your home. Whatever the need, one of the best things you can do is to get your mind off yourself and help meet somebody else's need. Sow some seeds of happiness. That's the way to receive a huge harvest.

The Bible says, "In times of difficulty, trust in the Lord and do good" (see Psalm 37:1–3). It's not enough to say, "God, I trust You. I know You are going to meet all my needs." That's like the farmer not planting any seeds and expecting a fabulous harvest. Scripture says there are two things we must do in times of trouble. First, we must trust in the Lord: and second, we must go out and do something good. Go out and sow some seeds. If you need a financial miracle, go buy somebody a cup of coffee tomorrow morning, or give a little extra in the offering at church. If you don't have any money, do some physical work for somebody; mow somebody's lawn, pull some weeds, wash their windows. Make someone a pie. Do *something* to get some seed in the ground.

When you make other people happy, God will make sure that your life is filled with joy.

If you are lacking in friends, don't sit at home alone month after month, feeling sorry for yourself. Go to the nursing home and find someone else who is lonely whom you can befriend. Go to the hospital and find somebody you can cheer up. If you'll start sowing seeds of friendship, God will bring somebody great into your life. When you make other people happy, God will make sure that your life is filled with joy.

We need to be more seed-oriented than need-oriented. In your time of need, don't sit around thinking about what you lack. Think about what kind of seed you can sow to get yourself out of that need.

In my book *Your Best Life Now*, I told a story about Lakewood Church's first building program. We didn't have much money, but there was a little Spanish church down the street that had plans to construct a new sanctuary, too. One Sunday morning my dad got up and announced to the congregation that we were going to take up a special offering, not for our new building, but for that little Spanish church. Several thousand dollars came in that morning, and we sent the check straight down the road. The truth is, we needed the money more than they did, but Daddy understood it was more important that we get some seed in the ground. Amazingly, it wasn't long before we had all the money we needed to get to work on our building project. We built that structure, plus several others, and down through the years, we've lived by that principle: In the time of need, sow a seed.

❧ Today's Prayer for Your Best Life Now ❧

Today, O Lord, I choose to focus on the needs of others rather than my own. I believe that as I plant seeds of goodness in other people's lives, You will do something similar in my own life. Thank You, Father, for the blessings that are coming!

SOW A SPECIAL SEED

SCRIPTURE READING FOR YOUR BEST LIFE NOW 2 Corinthians 9:1–15

Every man according as he purposeth in his heart, so let him give; not grudgingly, or of necessity: for God loveth a cheerful giver.

2 CORINTHIANS 9:7 KJV

SOME FIRST-CENTURY CHRISTIANS were struggling to survive in the Greek town of Corinth. The Bible says, "The people were in deep poverty and deep trouble" (see 2 Corinthians 8:2). What did they do in their time of need? Did they complain and pout? Did they say, "God, why do we have so much trouble coming against us?" Not at all. The Scripture records, "In the midst of their great trouble, they stayed full of joy and they gave generously to others." Notice they sowed a seed in their time of need. They knew if they would help to meet other people's needs, God would meet theirs.

In your times of difficulty, do just what they did. Number one, stay full of joy. Number two, go out and sow a seed. Help someone else, and you will be helped.

The Bible says, "Give generously, for your gifts will return to you later. Divide your gifts among many, for in the days ahead you yourself may need much help" (Ecclesiastes 11:1–2 TLB). Notice, God is giving us a principle here that will cause us to have our needs supplied during those tough times that occasionally come.

Give generously right now, because in the future you may need some help.

God is keeping a record of every good deed you've ever done. He is keeping a record of every seed you've ever sown. And in your time of need, He will make sure that somebody is there to help you. Your generous gifts will come back to you. God has seen every smile you've ever given to a hurting person. He's observed every time you went out of the way to lend a helping hand. God has witnessed when you have given sacrificially, giving even money that perhaps you needed desperately for yourself or your family. God is keeping those records. Some people will tell you that it doesn't make any difference whether you give or not, or that it doesn't do any good. But don't listen to those lies. God has promised that your generous gifts will come back to you (see Luke 6:38).

Put some action behind your prayers. If you are believing for a promotion at work, don't just say, "God, I'm counting on You." Certainly, you should pray, but do more than pray. Go out and feed the poor, or do something to get some seed in the ground that God can bless. Your gifts will go up as a memorial before God.

Perhaps you are hoping to buy a new home or to get out of debt. Sow a special seed that relates to your specific need. We can't buy God's goodness, but we can exercise our faith through our giving.

God has witnessed when you have given sacrificially.

Victoria and I have proved this principle again and again in our lives, but one of the most memorable incidents took place early in our marriage when we decided that we wanted to sell our townhome and buy a house. For six or eight months, we never received a serious offer. At the time, we were making double mortgage payments on the townhome, in an attempt to pay the principal down sooner. We decided to make the one required payment, and we'd sow the second part of that money as a seed, giving it to God's work, trusting for God's favor. We did that faithfully for several months, believing for the townhome to sell.

God not only brought us a buyer, but He did more than we could ask or think. We sold our townhouse for even more than we were hoping for!

The Scripture says, "When we give, God is able to make it all up to us by giving us everything we need and more so there will be not only enough for our needs, but we will have plenty left over so that we can give joyfully to others" (see 2 Corinthians 9:8). God has promised us that when we give, He will give back to us, then add some more.

Maybe you are in a situation similar to the one Victoria and I were in, where you are praying and believing and hoping for something to change, but thus far, nothing has happened. Perhaps you need to sow a special seed. Sow your time. Sow a special offering. Do something out of the ordinary as an expression of your faith. If you will do that, God will pour out His favor in a new way.

Friend, if you want to live your best life now, don't hoard what God has given you. Learn to sow it in faith. Remember, when you give, you are preparing the way for God to meet your needs today and in the future.

❧ Today's Prayer for Your Best Life Now ❧

Father, I want to do something out of the ordinary in the realm of giving, something that will stretch my faith, and cause me to know that when the answer comes, it is directly attributable to You and Your blessing on my willingness to give.

PART SEVEN

CHOOSE TO BE HAPPY

CHOOSE TO BE HAPPY TODAY

SCRIPTURE READING FOR YOUR BEST LIFE NOW   John 14:13–31

Peace I leave with you; My peace I give to you; not as the world gives do I give to you. Do not let your heart be troubled, nor let it be fearful.

JOHN 14:27 NASB

IT IS A simple yet profound truth: Happiness is a choice. When you get up in the morning, you can choose to be happy and enjoy that day, or you can choose to be unhappy and go around with a sour attitude. It's up to you. If you make the mistake of allowing your circumstances to dictate your happiness, then you risk missing out on God's abundant life.

You might as well choose to be happy and enjoy your life! When you do that, not only will you feel better, but your faith will cause God to show up and work wonders. God knows that we have difficulties, struggles, and challenges. But it was never His intention for us to live one day "on cloud nine," and the next day down in the dumps, defeated and depressed because we have problems. God wants us to live consistently. He wants us to enjoy every single day of our lives.

To do so, you must learn to live in today, one day at a time; better yet, make the most of this moment. It's good to have a big-picture outlook, to set goals, to establish budgets and make plans, but if you're always living in the future, you're never really enjoying the present in the way God wants you to.

When we focus too much on the future, we are often frustrated because we don't know what's coming. Naturally, the uncertainty increases our stress level and creates a sense of insecurity. We need to understand, though, that God has given us the grace to live today. He has not yet given us tomorrow's grace. When we get to tomorrow, we'll have the strength to make it through. God will give us what we need. But if we're worried about tomorrow right now, we are bound to be frustrated and discouraged.

Choose to start enjoying your life right now.

By an act of your will, choose to start enjoying your life right now. Learn to enjoy your family, your friends, your health, your work; enjoy everything in your life. Happiness is a decision you make, not an emotion you feel. Certainly there are times in all our lives when bad things happen, or things don't turn out as we had hoped. But that's when we must make a decision that we're going to be happy in spite of our circumstances.

"Joel, I can't do that. I'm just a real high-strung person," you may say. "I get upset easily." No—you can do whatever you want to do. God said He would never let us go through something that is too difficult for us to handle (see 1 Corinthians 10:13). And if your desire is great enough, you can stay calm and cool no matter what comes against you in life.

God gives us His peace on the inside, but it's up to us to make use of that peace. Especially in the pressure points of life, we have to learn how to tap into God's supernatural peace. The way you do that is by making a conscious choice, a calculated decision if you will, choosing to stay happy.

I was reminded of this choice one day when Victoria took my car to the car wash for me. At the time, I had a white 1995 Lexus that formerly belonged to my dad. Even though the car was getting old, it hardly had a scratch on it so it looked much newer.

On this day, Victoria drove it through our usual car wash—one of those with supposedly supersoft brushes that barely touch the car. Unfortunately, something was slightly out of alignment, because not only did it take the dirt off my car, it put a scratch from the front bumper all the way up the hood and over the roof to the back windshield!

When I saw the damages, I knew immediately that I had to make a decision. Was I going to get angry and allow this accident to steal my peace and my joy? Or was I going to rule over my emotions and not allow myself to be upset and agitated? Was I going to keep my peace, knowing that God was still in control?

I had to admit, the scratch was awful. But as I ran my fingers over the scratch from hood to trunk, I decided to look at the bright side. I said to Victoria, "Well, I guess I'm the only guy in Houston who's got a Lexus with a racing stripe right down the center."

When negative things happen to us, no matter how much we yell and scream, murmur and complain, it's not going to make anything better. I knew no matter how depressed I got about that car, or how much I flew off the handle at the car-wash people, it wasn't going to make that scratch go away. I decided that I might as well keep my peace. I might as well stay happy.

The Bible says we are like a mist, a vapor; we're here for a moment, then we're gone (see James 4:14). Life is flying by, so don't waste another moment of your precious time being angry, unhappy, or worried. The psalmist said, "This is the day which the LORD has made; let us rejoice and be glad in it" (Psalm 118:24 NASB). Notice, he didn't say, "Tomorrow, I will be happy." He didn't say, "Next week, when I don't have so many problems, I'm going to rejoice." No, he said, "*This* is the day." This is the day that God wants you to choose to be happy.

∞ Today's Prayer for Your Best Life Now ∞

Father, when things happen that would normally bother me, help me to put my foot down and say, "No, I'm not going to let that take my peace. I'm going to rule over my emotions. I'm not going to allow myself to get upset and aggravated. I'm going to choose to be happy."

BELIEVING THROUGH THE DRY SEASON

Trust in the LORD with all thine heart; and lean not unto thine own understanding. In all thy ways acknowledge him, and he shall direct thy paths.

PROVERBS 3:5–6 KJV

THINGS MAY NOT be perfect in your life, but if you hope to get to where you want to go, you must be happy right where you are. Many people assume that they are not going to be happy until their circumstances change—until their spouse changes, or until they get a bigger house, or until they get rid of all their problems.

Don't make that mistake. Enjoy your life right where you are. Maybe you have some major obstacles in your path, but being discouraged is not going to make anything better. You need to realize that God is in control of your life. He's directing your steps, and He has you exactly where He wants you.

The apostle Paul said, "I have learned how to be content in every situation whether I'm abased or abounding; whether I've got a lot or whether I don't have too much" (see Philippians 4:11–12). He was saying, "I've made a decision that I'm going to live my life happy." Now "content" doesn't mean we don't want to see change. It doesn't mean we simply sit back in neutral and accept everything as it comes. No, I like the way The Amplified Bible states Philippians 4:11: "I have learned how to be content (satisfied to the point where I am not disturbed or disquieted) in whatever state I am."

That's the key. You don't have to get upset because your circumstances are not exactly what you want them to be. Keep in mind that God will not allow a difficulty to come into your life, unless He has a purpose for it. You may not understand His purpose right now, but that's okay. God's ways are not our ways. If you'll keep the right attitude, God has promised He will turn that situation around in your favor, and you will come out better off than you were before.

We all go through dry seasons in our lives, times when we don't see anything happening. Maybe you've been praying and believing, but your prayers aren't being answered; or, you're giving, but you don't seem to be getting anything in return. Maybe you are doing your best to treat people right; you're going the extra mile to help others, but nobody is going out of their way to help you.

What's going on? Is God's Word a lie? Do these principles not work?

No, these dry seasons are proving grounds. God wants to see how you are going to respond. What kind of attitude will you have when you are doing the right thing, but the wrong thing keeps happening to you?

I've often told the story of how my father was the successful pastor of a large congregation that had just built a brand-new sanctuary. Daddy was on the state board for his denomination, and was on his way up in the church hierarchy.

But about that time, my sister Lisa was born with a birth injury, something similar to cerebral palsy. That was one of the darkest hours of my parents' lives. Mom and Dad searched the Scriptures, and they discovered that God is a good God and a healing God. They began to pray and believe that He could heal my sister Lisa. As their eyes were opened to the truth of Scripture, Daddy preached with a new fire and a new enthusiasm. He had a message of hope and healing, faith and victory. He thought everybody would be excited about the new things he was learning from the Scripture, but much to his surprise, the leaders of the congregation were opposed to Daddy's new emphasis. The idea of a contemporary, miracle-working God made them a bit uncomfortable.

The division was so severe, my heartbroken father eventually left that church and had to start all over. He and ninety other people went down the street to an abandoned feed store, an old rundown, dirty building that had holes in the floor. But they cleaned it up, and on Mother's Day, 1959, they opened Lakewood Church.

Now, here's where many people miss something important in the story. Most people think that the church just took off, that it grew quickly into the mega-church we know now as Lakewood Church. But it didn't happen that way. Daddy and his tiny congregation were still in that little abandoned feed store that held two hundred people nearly thirteen years later. The congregation didn't grow fast. In fact, in thirteen years, it hardly grew at all. It was an extremely dry season in my father's life.

Daddy had been accustomed to speaking to thousands and thousands of people all over the world. He was comfortable with success. Now, he was laboring in obscurity with a small congregation. By outward appearances, his efforts seemed a waste of his time. It didn't seem as though anything significant was happening. But God was doing a work in my father. He was getting him prepared for a greater ministry. And those thirteen years were a proving ground. That period in my father's life, and in the life of Lakewood Church, was a time of testing.

God is preparing you for greater things.

Daddy faithfully preached to those ninety people just as he had preached to the thousands. He put his heart and soul into it. He didn't let it bother him that he was preaching in a former feed store, rather than the big beautiful sanctuary he had helped to build. He knew if he remained faithful in the tough times, God would promote him. Sure enough, that's exactly what happened. Today, the overflowing joy and enthusiasm of the millions of people who have been touched, and the thousands of lives that have been transformed through the ministry of Lakewood Church, are a testimony to the faithfulness of one man who wouldn't give up during the dry seasons.

When you go through a dry season, a long period of time when you don't see anything good happening, just stay faithful; keep a smile on your face, and keep doing what you know is right. God is preparing you for greater things.

✕ Today's Prayer for Your Best Life Now ✕

Oh, God, it's relatively easy to be happy when everything is going well in my life. Help me to be just as happy and positive in my outlook when things aren't going so well. Bring me through the dry wilderness experiences having learned the lessons You want me to know.

GOD'S GUIDANCE WORKS

The LORD will continually guide you, and satisfy your desire in scorched places, and give strength to your bones; and you will be like a watered garden, and like a spring of water whose waters do not fail.

ISAIAH 58:11 NASB

Isn't it interesting that we believe God is guiding us as long as we are getting what we want and we're "living on the mountaintop," relatively unscathed by the warp and woof of life in the valley below. But we need to understand that the Lord is directing our steps even when it seems things are not going our way. You may be in a stressful situation today. You may be living with a spouse or a child who is difficult to get along with. Or perhaps because of favoritism or politics at the office, you are not being treated fairly, or possibly you are having to work two jobs in order to make ends meet. You may be thinking, *This doesn't seem right. God, I don't understand it.*

The Scripture says, "Since the Lord is directing our steps, why try to figure out everything that happens along the way?" (see Proverbs 20:24). Friend, you are never going to understand everything you go through in life or why certain things come against you. You simply must learn to trust God anyway. You must learn to keep a good attitude in the midst of the chaos and confusion, knowing that God is still in control.

In *Your Best Life Now*, I told the story of two former college basketball players who were headed to Kenya to work on a mis-

God knows what He's doing.

sions project back in the late 1990s. But they were delayed and missed their connecting flight. They were extremely disappointed, as the next flight wasn't for eight or nine hours. They were a bit irritated and said so.

When it finally came time for the next flight to leave, there were no seats available except in first class. The airline seated the two big fellows right up at the front of the plane, with plenty of legroom, so they were happy about that. But about midway through that flight, the plane took a nose-dive and started streaking toward the ground at full throttle. People aboard the plane screamed frantically as the flight attendants scrambled to keep the passengers from panicking. They thought for sure they were going to die.

The two big basketball players maintained their wits enough to pray: "God, we really don't understand this, but please use our lives somehow."

About that time, they heard some noise that sounded like a struggle in the cockpit. A flight attendant opened the cockpit door, and there was a deranged man—a big man who stood over seven feet tall—attacking the pilots and trying to gain control of the plane. The pilots were desperately trying to stop the madman, but they didn't have a chance.

When the two basketball players saw what was happening, they wrestled the attacker to the ground and pulled him out of the cockpit. By the time they were able to subdue him, the plane had fallen all the way from 30,000 feet to less than 4,000 feet. Had the pilots not been able to regain control, within seconds the plane would have crashed, most likely killing everyone aboard and possibly people on the ground.

Sometimes God will put you in an uncomfortable situation so you can help somebody else. God delayed those two young men on purpose. He put them in first class, right up front, so they could help save that entire plane. God knows what He's doing. He can see the big picture; He can see the future. And He has you exactly where He wants you today. Quit questioning Him and start trusting Him. Just know that God is in control. He has your best interests at heart. Trust Him today to direct your steps, and to cause you to be right where you need to be at just the right time.

✑ Today's Prayer for Your Best Life Now ✑

Thank You, Father, that even in the uncomfortable spots in life, I can have confidence that You are aware of me, that You care about what is happening to me, and that You have a plan to bring good into my life and through my life as a result.

THE PERSON GOD BLESSES

SCRIPTURE READING FOR YOUR BEST LIFE NOW   Colossians 3:9–25

Whatever you do, do your work heartily, as for the Lord rather than for men, knowing that from the Lord you will receive the reward of the inheritance. It is the Lord Christ whom you serve.

COLOSSIANS 3:23–24 NASB

WHY IS IT that some people are so blessed and continue to prosper and get ahead, while others remain in ruts of their own making? There may be many factors, of course, but one thing is for sure: God doesn't bless mediocrity. He blesses excellence. The Scripture says, "Whatever you do, work at it with your whole heart, not unto men, but do it unto God knowing that God will reward you" (see Colossians 3:23–24). Notice, whatever we do, we should give it our best effort and do it as if we were doing it for God. If we'll work with that standard in mind, God promises to reward us.

What does it mean to be a person of excellence and integrity?

A person of excellence and integrity goes the extra mile to do what's right. He keeps his word even when it's difficult. People of excellence arrive at work on time. They give their employers a full day's work; they don't leave early or call in sick when they are not. When you have an excellent spirit, it shows up in the quality of your work, and the attitude with which you do it.

If you want to live your best life now, start aiming for excellence and integrity in everything you do, doing a little bit more than you are required to do. If you are supposed to be at work at eight o'clock, get there ten minutes early and stay ten minutes late. Go the extra mile. A lot of people show up at work fifteen minutes late, then they wander around the office, go get some coffee, and finally get to their desk or workstation thirty minutes later. They spend half the day engaged in personal telephone calls, playing games, or sending jokes on the Internet, and then they wonder, *God, why don't You ever bless me? Why don't I ever get a promotion?*

The answer is easy to figure out. God doesn't bless mediocrity. God blesses excellence and integrity.

"But Joel, everybody's doing it. Everybody gets to work late at my office. Everybody surfs the Internet when the boss is gone. Everybody takes extra-long lunch breaks."

Maybe so, but you are not like everybody else! You are called to live a life of excellence. You represent Almighty God. How you live, how you conduct your business and do your work is all a reflection on our God.

Start making the more excellent choices in every area of life, even in mundane matters such as paying your bills on time. In everything you do, attempt to represent God well. For instance, you may be driving a car that hasn't been washed in six weeks. Your trunk or backseat may be filled with so much junk—everything from your sports equipment to your office equipment— you can barely close the door! I'm not

Take pride in what God has given you.

condemning anybody—Victoria and I have children, too—and sometimes our car looks like a storm hit it. But I don't like driving a car like that. Not only does it represent God poorly, but it makes me feel unkempt, undisciplined, sloppy, and less than my best. Many times before I leave the house, I'll take a couple of minutes and clean out the car, not because I want to impress my friends, but because I feel better driving a clean car. You need to take pride in what God has given you.

You may say, "Well, Joel, I'm just driving an old clunker. No use in my washing that thing."

No, if you will start taking care of what God has given you, He'll be more likely to give you something better. Similarly, you may not live in a big, new, beautiful home. You may have an older, smaller home, but at least you can keep it clean and looking nice. Make sure it looks like a person of excellence lives there.

God's people are people of excellence. They stand out from the crowd because they choose to do things well. You may be in a situation today where everybody around you is compromising their integrity or taking the easy way out. Don't let that rub off on you. Be the one to have an excellent spirit. Do your work well, take care of the resources that God has given you, and live in such a manner that when people see you, they will be attracted to your God.

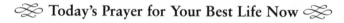

Today's Prayer for Your Best Life Now

Let my life be a positive reflection of You, O Lord. In everything I say and do, by the way I dress to the way I take care of my personal possessions, I pray that You will receive honor from my life.

BEING A PERSON OF INTEGRITY

Scripture Reading for Your Best Life Now   Matthew 25:14–30

Quick! Catch all the little foxes before they ruin the vineyard of your love, for the grapevines are all in blossom.

Song of Songs 2:15 NLT

Have you ever felt as though somebody was watching you? Guess what? Whether you realize it or not, people *are* watching you. They're watching how you dress, how you take care of your home, how you treat other people. They're watching you at play and at work. They are trying to determine whether your words and your walk—your lifestyle—are consistent. What do they see? Are you a good representation of our God? Are you striving for excellence? Or are you compromising in so-called insignificant areas?

God wants us to be people of integrity, people of honor, people who are trustworthy. A person of integrity is open and honest. He doesn't have any hidden agendas or ulterior motives. A person of integrity is true to his word. He keeps his commitments. He doesn't need a legal contract to force him to fulfill his promises; his word is his bond. People of integrity are the same in private as they are in public. They don't go out and treat their friends and coworkers kindly and then go home and treat their family rudely or disrespectfully. No, when you have integrity, you'll do what's right whether anybody is watching or not.

Every day our integrity is tested. If the bank teller gives you too much money in return, are you going to have integrity and go back and make things right? Or are you going to go out of there saying, "Thank You, Jesus! You did it again!"

Do you call in sick at work so you can stay home and take care of your personal business, go to the beach, or go play golf? When the boss asks how things are going, do you inflate the figures in your favor? When the phone rings and it's somebody you don't want to talk to, do you tell your child to lie? "Tell them I'm not home!"

"Oh, Joel, that's just a little white lie," some people say. "It's not hurting anything." No, lies are not color coded in the Bible. In God's sight, there is no such thing as a white, gray, or black lie. A lie is a lie. If you're not telling the truth, that's being dishonest. Sooner or later, it will catch up to you. What you sow you will eventually reap.

Understand this: If you will lie about the little things, before long you'll lie about bigger things. We read about the large companies that have come tumbling down because of fraud and financial misdeeds. Those people didn't start off by stealing millions of dollars. Most likely, they started off compromising a hundred dollars here, a thousand dollars there. Then, when the opportunity came, they compromised millions. Don't kid yourself, if you will compromise in something small, eventually you will compromise in more serious matters. Compromise is a downhill slide. And theft is theft, whether it's a dollar, a thousand dollars, or a million dollars. If you're taking home your company's office supplies, that's being dishonest. If you're not giving your company a full day's work, that's not integrity. If you're having to stretch the truth in order to get that new account, that is deceit, and God won't bless that. We need to live honestly before our God and before other people. I heard somebody put it this way: "Don't do anything that you wouldn't feel comfortable reading about in the newspaper the next day."

If you don't have integrity, you will never reach your highest potential. Integrity is the foundation on which a truly successful life is built. Every time you compromise, every time you are less than honest, you are causing a slight crack in your foundation. If you continue compromising, that foundation will never be able to hold what God wants to build. You'll never have lasting prosperity if you don't first have integrity. Oh, you may enjoy some temporary success, but you'll never see the fullness of God's favor if you don't take the high road and make the more excellent choices. On the other hand, God's blessings will overtake us if we settle for nothing less than living with integrity.

Of course, we all want to prosper in life. But the real question is: Are we willing to pay the price to do the right thing? It's not always easy. Are we paying our honest debts? Are we being above board in our business decisions? Are we treating other people with respect and honor? Are we being true to our word? Integrity and prosperity are flip sides of the same coin. You can't have one without the other.

God may be reminding you about something such as paying a bill that you've swept under the rug. Maybe it's about getting to work on time consistently; maybe you know you should be more truthful in your business dealings. Start making things right. Step up to a higher level of integrity in those areas. God is calling us out of mediocrity and into excellence.

Integrity and prosperity are flip sides of the same coin.

The Bible says if we will be faithful in little things, then God will trust us with more (see Matthew 25:21). How can God trust me to do the right thing with millions of dollars, if I won't do the right thing with a hundred bucks? Yet how often have we heard of instances in which a person's upward progress was thwarted because of his or her mismanagement of something seemingly minor and insignificant?

You may not think it makes any difference when you don't pay your bills on time, or when you tell those "little white lies." You may think it doesn't make a difference if you treat your friends one way and your family another. But if you don't learn to pass those tests, God will not promote you. If you don't learn to do what's right in the little areas, God can't trust you with more. Remember, our lives are an open book before God. He looks at our hearts. He looks at our motives. God sees every time you go the extra mile to do what's right. He also sees the times that you compromise and take the easy way out.

Be open and honest and tell the whole truth. Learn to listen to your conscience. God put that inside you so you would have an inner rule by which to know right from wrong. When you start to compromise, you will hear that alarm go off in your conscience. Don't ignore it. Do what you know in your heart is the right thing.

Is somebody watching you? Oh, yes; people are watching, and so is your heavenly Father. Live this day to please Him, and you will be pleased with yourself.

❧ Today's Prayer for Your Best Life Now ❧

Father, help me to do the right thing whether anyone is watching or not. I know You see my actions, and beyond that, You know the motives of my heart. I want my words and deeds to be pleasing to You.

---

1. toil — hard work.
2. toll — fare, fee
3. replenish — fill
4. zest — passion, eagerness
5. dwindle — diminish, make small
6. stagnant — not moving/changing
7. mamma [ɛmɛmɑ] 엄마 젖
8. lag — 꾸물거리다, 뒤처지다

9. zeal — passion
10. aglow → on fire, 흥분된 몸짓으로
11. dawdle — waste time, 꾸물거리다/빈둥거리다
12. ethic → 윤리
13. contagious → 감염되는, 전염하는
14. alternate → 번갈아 바뀌다, 교대하다, 번갈아 하다
15. caustic → sarcastic
16. cynical (비꼬는)
→ 비꼬는, 냉소적인

STAYING INSPIRED

SCRIPTURE READING FOR YOUR BEST LIFE NOW   Psalm 150:1–6

Never be lazy in your work, but serve the Lord enthusiastically.

ROMANS 12:11 NLT

PRESSURE, TENSION, STRESS! The daily toils of modern life constantly threaten to take a toll on our enthusiasm, causing it to quickly evaporate if it is not continually replenished. It's not always easy to stay excited and inspired in the middle of a long journey. You probably know some people who have lost their passion. They've lost their zest for life. Once they were excited about the future. They were excited about their dreams, but they've lost their fire.

Perhaps even in your own life you've seen evidence of dwindling enthusiasm. Maybe at one time you were excited about your marriage. You were deeply in love, so full of passion, but now your marriage has become stale and stagnant. Or maybe you were excited about your job. You loved going to work, but recently, it's become dull, routine, and boring. Maybe at one time you were excited about serving God. You couldn't wait to get to church. You loved reading your Bible, praying, and spending time with fellow believers. But lately you've been thinking, *I don't know what's wrong with me. I don't have any drive. I don't have any passion. I'm just going through the motions.*

The truth is, much of life is routine, and we can become stagnant if we're not careful. We need to stir ourselves up, to replenish our supply of God's good gifts on a daily basis. Like the Israeli people in the wilderness who had to gather God's miraculous provisions of manna afresh each morning, we, too, cannot get by on yesterday's supply. We need fresh enthusiasm each day. The word *enthusiasm* derives from two Greek words, *en theos*, meaning "inspired by God." Our lives need to be inspired, infused, filled afresh with God's goodness every day.

> Are you
> *aglow* with
> God's
> presence in
> your life?

Make a decision that you are not going to live another day without the joy of the Lord in your life; without love, peace, and passion; without being excited about your life. And understand that you don't have to have something extraordinary happening in your life to be excited. You may not live in the perfect environment or have the perfect job or the perfect marriage, but you can still choose to live each day with enthusiasm. The Scripture says, "Never lag in zeal, but be aglow and on fire, serving the Lord enthusiastically" (see Romans 12:11). Do those terms describe your life? Are you *aglow* with God's presence in your life? Are you *on fire* with enthusiasm? You can be! When you awaken in the morning, do you get up with passion to meet the day? Are you excited about your dreams? Do you go to work each day with enthusiasm?

"Well, I don't really like my job," someone complains. "I can't stand driving in the traffic. I don't like the people I work around."

If that sounds familiar, you need to change your attitude. You should be grateful that you even have a job. You need to appreciate and stay excited about the opportunities God has given you. Wherever you are in life, make the most of it and be the best that you can be. If your assignment right now is to raise your children, do it with passion. Do it with enthusiasm. Don't get up and say,

"Humph! My friends are out doing something significant, something important, something exciting. All I'm doing is taking care of these kids."

A mother's work is one of the most important jobs in the whole world. But you have to keep up your enthusiasm. You may not have somebody patting you on the back or cheering you on. Your day may not be filled with extraordinary events. There are diapers to change, children to feed, clothes to be washed and pressed, housework that needs to be done; routine, mundane chores that seem to start over the moment you complete them. But in the midst of the ordinary, you can choose to have an extraordinary attitude toward your work. The Scripture tells us to do everything we do with our whole hearts, "to never lag in zeal."

If you work outside the home, don't give your employer a half-hearted effort. Don't dawdle on the telephone, wasting your employer's time and money. If you are digging a ditch, don't spend half the day leaning on your shovel; do your work with excellence and enthusiasm!

"Well, they don't pay me enough, anyway. I shouldn't have to work very hard."

You won't be blessed with that kind of attitude. God wants you to give it everything you've got. Be enthusiastic. Set an example. Do your work with such excellence that others will be impressed with your God merely by observing your positive work ethic.

We should be so excited, and so full of joy that other people will want what we have. Ask yourself, "Is the way I'm living attractive and contagious? Will my attitudes, the words I speak, my expressions, the way I handle challenges and setbacks, cause anybody to want what I have?" In other words, are you drawing people to God because of your joy, your friendliness, your enthusiasm, your attitude of faith? Or do you alienate people, turning them away because you're perpetually negative, discouraged, caustic, or cynical? Nobody enjoys being around a person like that. If you want to point people to God, or simply to a better way of living, have some enthusiasm and be excited about life.

❧ Today's Prayer for Your Best Life Now ❧

Father, please let my enthusiasm for life be contagious; may I live in such a way that causes other people to want to know You and how they can discover a different, better quality of life now and forever.

1. embers   재. 타다남은것
2. rekindle   다시 불붙이다
3. stir up   일으키다, 북받치다
4. be prone to ~하기 쉬운
5. squelch = squeeze = press to get st out
6. deadbeat
7. murky   흐린, 흐릿한.

KEEP IT GOING

SCRIPTURE READING FOR YOUR BEST LIFE NOW   Hebrews 12:1–14

"I know the plans I have for you," declares the LORD, *"plans to prosper you and not to harm you, plans to give you hope and a future."*

JEREMIAH 29:11 NIV

ONE OF MY favorite stories in *Your Best Life Now* involves a traffic policeman who worked by the Galleria, one of the busy shopping areas in Houston. During rush hour, the traffic would be so badly backed up, it was not uncommon to have to wait ten or fifteen minutes just to get through one light. Observing people in their cars, it was plain to see that they were irritated about having to wait so long. But when they approached the policeman, their whole attitude changed.

This officer didn't simply direct traffic. He put on a show! He was so enthusiastic, just watching him was entertaining. It was obvious that he loved what he was doing. He was practically dancing as he directed that traffic, with both arms waving wildly, his hands gesturing, his feet shuffling all through the intersection, all at the same time!

Amazingly, after inching along in the traffic jam for ten or fifteen minutes, many drivers would pull over into nearby parking lots just to watch the traffic officer perform. He was *enthusiastic*.

He wasn't just showing up for work. He wasn't just going through the motions. No, he was passionately fulfilling his destiny.

That's the way you and I should be. Don't just go through the motions in life. Have some enthusiasm. Choose to be happy; live with excellence and integrity, and put a spring in your step. Put a smile on your face, and let the world know that you are enjoying the life God has given you!

Friend, if you want to see God's favor, do everything with your whole heart. Do it with passion and some fire. Not only will you feel better, but that fire will spread, and soon other people will want what you have. Do you want your life to make an impact? You can change the atmosphere of your home or your entire office with a little bit of enthusiasm.

In the New Testament, the apostle Paul encouraged his young coworker Timothy: "Fan the flame. Rekindle the embers. Stir up the gift that is within you" (see 2 Timothy 1:6). Paul was reminding his understudy to live with enthusiasm. Give it your all. Don't settle for mediocrity. Stir yourself up; rekindle that fire.

You may have to live or work around people who are prone to being negative, who tend to drag you down. But don't let them throw water on your fire. Don't let their lack of enthusiasm squelch your passion. If you live with a deadbeat spouse, make a decision that you're going to be happy and enthusiastic anyway. If you work around people who are always negative, try to overcome that negativity by being positive, encouraging, and uplifting. Fan your flame more than usual to make sure the fire doesn't go out.

When everybody else is down and defeated, when you are all alone with nobody nearby to encourage you, simply encourage yourself. Your attitude should be: *It doesn't matter what anybody else does or doesn't do, I'm going to live my life with enthusiasm! I'm going to stay on fire. I'm going to be aglow. I'm going to be passionate about seeing my dreams come to pass.*

People who see me on television sometimes write to me, saying,

"Joel, why do you always smile so much? Why are you so happy? Why are you so enthusiastic?"

"I'm glad you asked!" I respond, and that opens the door for me to tell them about my relationship with God, and how they can have a relationship with Him as well.

Some guy stopped me on the street in New York City and said, "Hey, aren't you that smiling preacher?"

I laughed and said, "I guess so. That's me. I'm the smiling preacher." I take that as a compliment. Yes, I'm guilty of being happy! I'm guilty of being excited about the future. I'm guilty of living each day with enthusiasm.

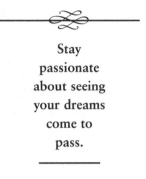

Stay passionate about seeing your dreams come to pass.

That's what it means to stay full of zeal. Stay passionate about seeing your dreams come to pass. Stay on fire and aglow. Whatever you do, do it with enthusiasm!

The Bible says, "If you are willing and obedient, you shall eat the good of the land" (Isaiah 1:19 NKJV). Notice, we have to be more than obedient; we must be willing—willing to do the right thing, willing to live with a good attitude and with enthusiasm.

Friend, God doesn't want you to drag through life defeated and depressed. No matter what you've been through, no matter whose fault it was, no matter how impossible your situation may look, the good news is that God wants to turn it around and restore everything that has been stolen from you. He wants to restore your marriage, your family, your career. He wants to restore those broken dreams. He wants to restore your joy and give you a peace and happiness you've never known before. Most of all, He wants to restore your relationship with Him. God wants you to live a satisfied life.

God doesn't want you simply to feel a little better for a few days. No, God is in the long-term restoration business. He wants you to have a life filled with an abundance of joy, an abundance of happiness. God doesn't want you simply to survive that marriage. God wants to turn it around and restore you with a strong, healthy, rewarding relationship. God doesn't want your business to merely make it through the murky economic waters. He wants your business to sail and to excel! When God restores, He always brings you out better, improved, increased, and multiplied. He has a vision of total victory for your life!

Hold on to that new, enlarged vision of victory that God has given you. Start expecting things to change in your favor. Dare to boldly declare that you are standing strong against the forces of darkness. You will not settle for a life of mediocrity!

Raise your level of expectancy. It's our faith that activates the power of God. Let's quit limiting Him with our small-minded thinking and start believing Him for bigger and better things. You can start today to live your best life now. Remember, if you obey God and are willing to trust Him, you will have the best this life has to offer—and more!

❧ Today's Prayer for Your Best Life Now ❧

Thank You, Father, for giving me this amazing, incredible life, and for making it possible to enjoy every part of it, even the tough times. Thank You for being my Future; I know You have good things in store. I will praise You now and forever for all that You have done for me!